A BOOK FOR
FAMILY
READING

BOOK 3

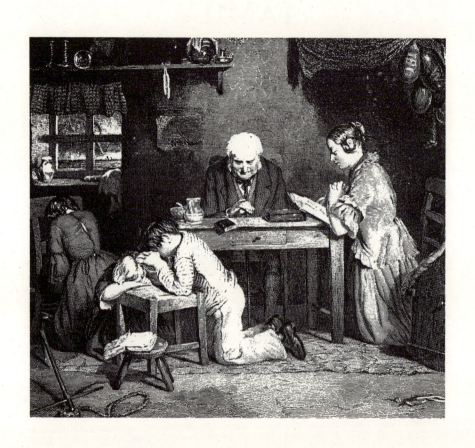

A BOOK FOR
FAMILY
READING

'One that didn't get away'
and other stories that teach biblical truths

Jim Cromarty

EP EVANGELICAL PRESS

EVANGELICAL PRESS
12 Wooler Street, Darlington, Co. Durham, DL1 1RQ, England

First published 1997

British Library Cataloguing in Publication Data available

ISBN 0 85234

Printed and bound by The Bath Press, Bath

To our daughters—
Vicki, Heather, Catherine and Lisa.

Contents

Preface

I have a lovely picture at home of a family gathered around the kitchen table (see frontispiece). Mum is kneeling at the kitchen table with an open Bible before her. Dad has his head bowed and is praying. The three young children are kneeling beside their chairs. The painting has a title: 'The Fisherman's Family — Evening Prayer'.

From the drawing it is easy to tell that the family is not wealthy. But they are rich in spiritual matters. God is being worshipped! All Christian families should gather for daily worship and I pray that your family carries out this important duty. The purpose for writing this book was to give parents a series of studies suitable for use in family worship.

Family members must be made aware of sin and the consequences of sin. And they must be shown the love of God as seen in the saving work of Jesus Christ. Thus it is that God has placed a great responsibility upon parents, especially fathers, to train their children in the ways of God. Paul spelt it out clearly: 'And you, fathers, do not provoke your children to wrath, but bring them up in the training and admonition of the Lord' (Ephesians 6:4).

Parents must set their children the example of godly living. Parents must take their children to worship services. Parents must teach their children of the love of God which is found in Jesus Christ. One of the greatest joys any parents can experience is the knowledge that their children have come to faith in Christ — faith which is 'the gift of God'. Pray that each member of your family might receive that precious 'gift' of God who 'so loved the world that he gave his only begotten Son, that whoever believes in him should not perish but have everlasting life' (John 3:16).

But, young people, you have the responsibility to come to Christ. You are responsible for your actions. Read your Bible. Pray to God pleading that he might send the Holy Spirit into your heart. When this happens you will be able to live the life of faith. And a true joy will be yours because eternal life has been planted in your heart.

May God be pleased to bless these writings to the hearts of all who read and listen.

Jim Cromarty

Who is God?

....**Read**..........
Isaiah 40:18-28

'God is Spirit, and those who worship him must worship in spirit and truth' (John 4:24).

I am learning how to use my computer. When I was choosing one, I was told that the Apple Macintosh was 'user-friendly'. Maybe I'm getting old, but I sometimes find even my 'user-friendly' computer difficult to control. When I turn on my machine a sign says, 'Welcome to Macintosh.' I have no idea how it works, but it does, and that is all that really matters.

I sometimes think about the intelligence of the people who put computers together and it is all beyond me. One young man I taught some years ago told me he built his own computer. I found that hard to believe, but I know that a computer has an intelligent discoverer and builder behind it. Looking at the universe about me, I see every sign of an intelligent builder. I gaze into the heavens at night and my mind tells me that all of this didn't just happen by accident. Behind the creation I can see there is a wise and powerful Being, who is God.

The Bible clearly tells us this and warns us that we must all recognize the existence of God: 'For since the creation of the world his invisible attributes are clearly seen, being understood by the things that are made, even his eternal power and Godhead, so that they are without excuse...' (Romans 1:20).

The creation has a Creator, and from his creation we can see the almighty power that was involved in bringing it about. We should also understand the great power that keeps the creation functioning. The sun hangs in space and the earth and other planets swing about it. The moon continues to revolve around the earth. The psalmist writes, 'The heavens declare the glory of God; and the firmament shows his handiwork' (Psalm 19:1). On the earth the rain falls, the seasons come and go and the trees and plants grow.

The creation speaks of the wisdom of God, for we can see that everything works together in a glorious way. The kindness and love of God are clearly seen in his provision for the needs of all his creatures. Surely, when we look at creation we can only say in amazement, 'O LORD, our Lord, how excellent is your name in all the earth!' (Psalm 8:9).

We can see the evidence for the existence of God, but we cannot see God. And how do we get to know more about this great Creator God? God has seen fit to reveal himself to us through his Word, the Bible. By reading the Bible we learn more and more about God.

We discover from our text that God is Spirit. This is important to know for then the first and second commandments make good sense. We read, 'You shall have no other gods before me. You shall not make for yourself any carved image, or any likeness of anything that is in heaven above, or that is in the earth beneath, or that is in the water under the earth; you shall not bow down to them nor serve them. For I, the LORD your God, am a jealous God...' (Exodus 20:3-5).

We are told here that God cannot be represented by anything we might make. As Jesus tells us in our text, 'God is Spirit...' In some parts of the world people make idols. They imagine what God is like; then they mould their god. After this they bow down and worship the idol they have made.

Some time ago my wife and I had a holiday in Thailand. There were many temples in that country and many idols were worshipped. On one tour we visited some floating markets. We travelled by boat along a canal till we came to a village built over the water. The shopkeepers there always had plenty of tourists, so they had a very big market. We could buy so many things, and all quite cheaply. It was very exciting!

My wife bargained for a lovely coloured cane hat as well as some toys for our grandchildren. But I saw an ebony elephant which represented one of the animals found in their temples. I thought it would look good on my study table, so I decided to buy it.

I approached the young Thai girl who had the small shop and asked if the beautiful black elephant was really made from ebony. She nodded her head, so I began to bargain. Before long I was carrying my ebony elephant and some other bits and pieces wrapped up in a plastic bag. I was very pleased with myself. I had bargained very well and I thought I had made an excellent buy.

Late that night, tired and weary, we returned to our hotel in Bangkok. We opened our purchases to show each other what we had bought. I showed my wife the lovely black ebony elephant which I had obtained so cheaply.

Val examined the elephant and asked, 'Didn't you say the elephant was carved from ebony?'

'Yes,' I replied. 'Isn't it great? It will look really good on my study table.'

Again Val looked closely at the elephant and then asked, 'Isn't ebony supposed to be black?'

'Sure,' I replied.

'Then why are there so many white spots and marks on this elephant? It looks as if the elephant has white between the toes. And look in the ears. There are white spots there too,' she said.

I suddenly had some terrible thoughts. 'Where?' I asked.

Val showed me spots of white here and there on the elephant. When I scratched my fingernail on the elephant's belly, the paint came off and white plastic was revealed. I almost hung my head in shame. My lovely 'ebony' elephant turned out to be a fake, and it wasn't so cheap after all.

And this is true of all idols. They are all fakes. They are made of wood, stone, gold — yes, and even plastic.

The psalmist has something to say about such gods:

Their idols are silver and gold,
The work of men's hands.
They have mouths, but they do not speak;
Eyes they have, but they do not see;
They have ears, but they do not hear;
Noses they have, but they do not smell;
They have hands, but they do not handle;
Feet they have, but they do not walk;
Nor do they mutter through their throat.
Those who make them are like them;
So is everyone who trusts in them

(Psalm 115:4-8).

The psalmist tells us who the true God is. He writes,

But our God is in heaven;
He does whatever he pleases

(Psalm 115:3).

Our God is Spirit. He fills the heavens and the earth. There is no place we can go where God is not present. He created the world and all things in it. He controls the world, and has revealed himself both in creation and through the written Word, which is our Bible.

But God has revealed himself in a more glorious way still. He has revealed himself to the world through his only begotten Son, Jesus Christ. In 2 Corinthians 4:4 Paul tells us that Christ is 'the image of God'. Then in Colossians 1:15 he writes of Christ, 'He is the image of the invisible God, the first-born over all creation.'

The apostle John tells us something about Christ when he writes, 'In the beginning was the Word [Christ], and the Word was with God, and the Word was God. He was in the beginning with God. All things were made through him, and without him nothing was made that was made' (John 1:1-3). This tells us that Christ is God and was always with God. We are also told that God created the world through his Son.

We worship one God, who is Spirit. But in the 'Godhead' the Bible tells us there are three persons: the Father, the Son and the Holy Spirit. Three persons, but one God — this is a mystery to our minds, but we are asked to believe all that God has revealed about himself.

And if you truly believe in God's revelation and trust in his Son Jesus Christ for your salvation, then you know that the Holy Spirit has already changed your heart and soul, and made it possible for you to believe and trust. Then as a new creature in Christ you will serve him and worship God. You will worship God in your spirit — your mind and soul. And you will worship God in 'truth' — that is, through his Son, Jesus Christ.

As you work your way through this book, you will, God willing, learn more and more about the almighty and glorious God who made all things and saved his people through the life and death of his beloved Son.

Activities

• •

1. Find Thailand on your atlas.
2. Who is Jesus and what special work has he done?
3. 'God is Spirit.' What does this mean?
4. What is an idol?

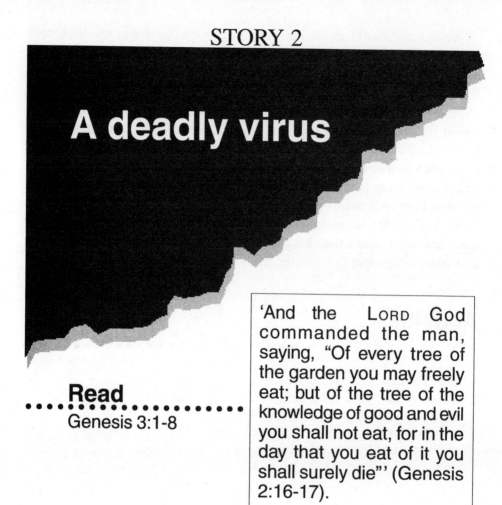

A deadly virus

Read

Genesis 3:1-8

'And the LORD God commanded the man, saying, "Of every tree of the garden you may freely eat; but of the tree of the knowledge of good and evil you shall not eat, for in the day that you eat of it you shall surely die"' (Genesis 2:16-17).

From the previous story you will have realized I have an Apple Macintosh computer. I purchased it several years ago. Beforehand I thought my biro and a piece of paper were all I needed. However, when I retired because of ill-health my wife said, 'Why not buy yourself a computer, Jim?'

I wasn't sure it would be a good idea. I didn't want one of those new-fangled things. I didn't understand computers and felt sure they just made people lazy. But my grandchildren urged me to get one. After all, they had computers at home and understood how to use them. Even Samantha, my three-year-old granddaughter, played games on the computer.

After much thinking and urging by the family I decided to buy one. I read books about computers. I didn't really understand the computer language, but my wife was so happy to think I would soon have a computer to occupy my time. The grandchildren said they would teach me how to use it. 'There's nothing to it, Pop!' was the cry. The pastor of our congregation, Pastor Peter, urged me to buy the 'user-friendly' Apple Macintosh.

Eventually, there on my study table was a computer, a printer and a CD-ROM machine. The salesman explained everything to me and left saying, 'Now don't forget to read the manual. If you have any problems just ring me and I'll tell you what to do.'

My brand-new computer worked wonders. Quite often it gave me instructions to carry out. Sometimes, however, I would have to ring Scott, my nine-year-old grandson, to find out what I should do. I still have no idea how it works, but it works wonderfully.

I had a new machine, there were no problems and it always did as I told it to do! It seemed just perfect. In fact it worked so well I was reminded of God creating the heavens and the earth. When God saw all that he had created, the Scriptures tell us that God declared everything to be 'very good'

(Genesis 1:31). There were no mistakes to be found in God's creation. There was no sin. Everything was perfect and worked perfectly. Adam and Eve had the most wonderful creation in which to live. They did as God commanded them and God walked and talked with them in the Garden of Eden.

After some months something went wrong with my computer. Instead of my smiling 'Welcome to Macintosh' sign, a very sad floppy disk appeared. Nothing worked. Every part of the computer had been affected by something. I tried to get it going again, but there was nothing I could do to get it to function. I rang the people from whom I had bought the computer and was told that I should bring the machine in and have it checked out. The result was that everything on my hard disk was lost. My great computer had a virus — it had become sick! But it was repaired and since then has not missed a beat.

What happened to my computer should remind you of what happened to Adam and Eve in the Garden of Eden. Satan tempted them to sin, and sin they did. If you have read your Bible passage for today you know the story. Adam and Eve were infected with a deadly virus — sin! Sin infected every part of them. Wicked thoughts came into their minds and they did terrible things. Their son Cain even killed his brother Abel. The sin virus ruined God's creation. Death entered the world and humans could do nothing to put things right with God.

Some have tried to live a life of total obedience to God, hoping that God would then save them. But no matter how hard they tried, they could never live a life of perfect obedience. Man's sin virus made perfect obedience impossible.

But just as only the computer shop could repair my computer, it was necessary for God himself to find a way to get rid of man's sin virus. Men and women were to be punished for their sins. But Jesus Christ, God's Son, came into the world and was punished by God in the place of his sinful people. He also did what no one else can do: he lived a life of perfect obedience to God, and this he did on behalf of his people. Jesus Christ is the only one able to destroy the sin virus that lives in the hearts of his people.

Reader, go to God and plead with him to send the Holy Spirit into your heart and use the blood of Christ to rid you of your sins. That is the only way to be put right with God. God has done what men and women could not do: he alone, through Jesus Christ his Son, has saved his people for eternal life in the new creation he will make when Christ returns.

Activities

● ●

1. What is a computer virus?
2. How did sin enter God's creation?
3. Why do you sin?
4. How can sinners be cleansed of their sin?

Little sins and big sins

Read
• •
2 Samuel 11:1-17

'When desire has conceived, it gives birth to sin; and sin, when it is full-grown, brings forth death' (James 1:15).

The Australian bush is well known for the many animals which live there. Two animals that are very unusual are the platypus and the spiny anteater or echidna. What makes them so unusual is that they are the only egg-laying mammals in the world. If you don't know much about these creatures you can read about them in an encyclopaedia.

However, there are other creatures found in the bush that are not so popular. Some spiders have very poisonous bites. There is the red-back spider, which really has a red spot on its back. A bite from this small spider can make a person very sick. Then there is the funnelweb spider, which usually lives underground. Sometimes they come into homes and hide in shoes or clothes left on the floor. A bite from this spider can kill!

But snakes are some of the bush creatures that I really do not like. Many snakes are quite harmless, but there are some that can bite and kill. I once saw a man who had been bitten by a red-belly black snake. He was brought into hospital while I was there and was violently ill for many hours.

Snakes usually live in the bush, but on occasions they have been known to come into homes. One of my friends once found a green tree snake in his bedroom. His wife refused to stay in the house for many days until a great search had been conducted to make sure there were no other snakes about.

Sometimes snakes wriggle underneath houses and then crawl up between the wooden walls. They can't get into the house, but it is very scary to be in a house, knowing a snake is not far away.

One day a good friend, whose name is Stewart, saw the tail of a snake poking out from under the brick foundations of his home. His wife Dorothy was there and pointed at the tail, lying in the sun. She whispered to her husband, 'You'll have to grab his tail and pull him out. It's only a small snake. I'll get the shovel and hit him when I can see enough of his back.'

Now Stewart was a brave man, but he whispered, 'No! I'm not that silly!' However, when Dorothy insisted, Stewart slowly put his hand down and grabbed the snake's tail. He was hoping it was a small snake, but as soon as he took hold, the snake tried to escape under the house. Dorothy lifted the shovel ready to hit the snake. She was really ready for action.

As Stewart pulled the snake, more and more of it appeared. It wasn't a small snake after all. In fact, by the time the snake was out it was about two metres long. And it was a red-belly black snake. Stewart was trembling with fear as he saw the snake getting bigger and bigger.

'It's a monster!' he shouted to Dorothy as she smashed the shovel down on the snake's head.

They both looked down at the snake in horror and amazement. Then Stewart said in a very trembling voice: 'I'll never do that again. It looked like a small snake when we saw the tip of its tail. It's like the iceberg: a little bit of ice floating on top of the water and the bigger part under the water.'

Now sin is like that snake. Just as the snake could have bitten Stewart or Dorothy and killed them, sin kills, for the Bible tells us that 'The wages of sin is death' (Romans 6:23). We are all sinners, and that is why every human dies.

And just as that snake looked small but was found to be very big, so sin too can grow. Small sins can become great sins. Coveting something which belongs to someone else is a sin. If you don't get your desires under control a greater sin could result: you might steal whatever it was that you longed to have as your own.

In today's Bible reading we read about King David, who saw a beautiful woman called Bathsheba.

King David should have been out on the battlefield with his men, but he had stayed in Jerusalem. It is very true that the devil finds work for idle hands to do. David was not doing what he should have been doing — he was in the wrong place.

When he saw Bathsheba, he should have turned away and gone about his business. But he decided to steal Bathsheba from her husband Uriah. Then, in order to have Bathsheba all to himself, he arranged for Uriah to be put in the most dangerous place of the battle. Uriah died, fighting for King David, not knowing that David had arranged for him to be killed. A terrible sin began with a look!

So it is that we must always be on our guard against sin. Every sin is an offence against our God. Some sins are worse than others. But let us always remember that little sins can grow into big sins — just as that snake became bigger and bigger as its tail was pulled from under the foundations of the house.

We all need to believe what the Bible tells us — that we were born into this world as sinners. That is why we sin! And we sin so easily!

Friend, if you are not a Christian, then ask God to change your heart. And when this happens, you will have a different attitude towards sin. Whereas you once loved your sins, now you will hate sin and by God's grace begin to live the life of righteousness.

Activities

● ●

1. Describe a platypus and find out all you can about this funny animal.
2. Who was King David?
3. Why does sin cause sinners to die?
4. Who was Uriah?

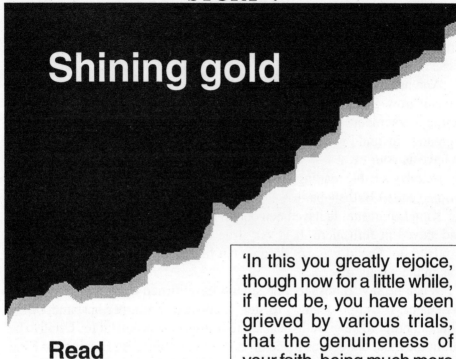

Shining gold

Read
Acts 6:7-8; 7:54-60

'In this you greatly rejoice, though now for a little while, if need be, you have been grieved by various trials, that the genuineness of your faith, being much more precious than gold that perishes, though it is tested by fire, may be found to praise, honour, and glory at the revelation of Jesus Christ' (1 Peter 1:6-7).

Some of you who are reading this chapter might believe that you are Christians. I would like to ask each of you this simple question: 'How do you know that you are a Christian?'

You might reply, 'I have faith in Jesus Christ, so I am a Christian.'

In that case I would like to ask you another question: 'How do you know that your faith is a saving faith?'

There are some passages of Scripture of which we should all take very special notice. Two such passages are: 'For as the body without the spirit is dead, so faith without works is dead also' (James 2:26); and 'Not everyone who says to me, "Lord, Lord," shall enter the kingdom of heaven, but he who does the will of my Father in heaven... And then I will declare to them, "I never knew you; depart from me, you who practise lawlessness!"' (Matthew 7:21,23). Here we are told that a saving faith must be followed by doing the will of God — by being obedient to God's commands. It is not enough to say you have faith in Christ; you must produce the evidence of that faith.

Christians are to love one another. It is not good enough for people to say they love others and then fail to show that love in the way they live. If a person doesn't show love for his or her brothers and sisters in Christ — indeed for all people — then that person's profession of faith is a lie. He or she is a hypocrite.

In today's reading we learn about Stephen, who was the first martyr of the Christian church. He proved that his faith was a living faith. He did the works of God and was willing to sacrifice his life for the Christ he loved and served. To die for love of Christ is the greatest sacrifice any Christian can make. When Christians suffer persecution, their faith is tested. If they stand firm despite the troubles they face it is a good proof that their faith is a living, saving faith.

In today's text we are reminded of this great truth. When difficult times  come, Christian faith is tried. In the hard times God's people trust themselves more and more to Christ their Saviour. This is true faith. In the hard times those people who pretend they are Christians usually turn from Christ and go back to the world they love. Jesus told the parable of the sower, where some of the seed fell on stony places. This seed grew, but soon died. Jesus likened this seed to the person who rejoiced when he heard the gospel, 'yet he has no root in himself, but endures only for a while. For when tribulation or persecution arises because of the word, immediately he stumbles' (Matthew 13:21).

When persecution comes God gives his people the grace they need to shine as his faithful saints in this world of darkness.

My brother searches for gold in his spare time. He finds nuggets of different sizes, but often the gold is embedded in rock and dirt. It is easy to get rid of the dirt, but to clean the gold properly John uses acid. This begins the purification process. But then for the gold to be really purified it must be melted. The refining process separates the waste material from the pure gold. Then the bright golden colour of the precious metal can easily be seen.

It is the same with our faith. The faith of God's people usually shines brightest in the days of persecution. Faithfulness to Christ shows the world that the faith of the saints is genuine.

How do you know that you have a saving faith in the Lord Jesus Christ? Well, look at your life and ask yourself, 'Do I, by the grace of God, obey the commandments of Christ?' Then watch your faithfulness in difficult times! Do you blame God when things go wrong? Do you tell your friends about Christ, even though they laugh at you when you claim to be a Christian?

The difficult days are to the Christian as heat is to metal. As the metal is purified by melting in the furnace, so faith is tested and purified through trials and temptations. If you are faithful to Christ in the difficult days, then this is a sign that your faith is real and that you belong to Christ.

Activities

● ●

1. To what precious metal does our text compare faith?
2. Why do you think gold is precious?
3. How do Christians know if their faith is a true faith?
4. Why do Christians obey Christ's commandments?

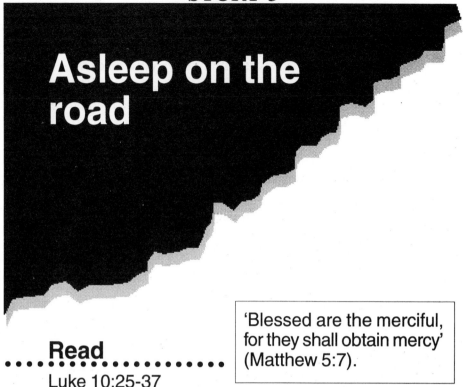

Asleep on the road

Read
•••••••••••••••••••
Luke 10:25-37

'Blessed are the merciful,
for they shall obtain mercy'
(Matthew 5:7).

We all have responsibilities for one another whether we are Christians or not. Our Bible reading for today teaches this very clearly. The Samaritan stepped down to help a Jew who hated him and his people. If you are a Christian you have a special responsibility to your brothers and sisters in Christ, but you are also to be like that Good Samaritan who helped a person who hated him.

In today's text Jesus speaks of Christians being merciful in their dealings with other people. And just as Christians show mercy, so for the sake of Jesus they receive mercy from God.

In some parts of the world human life is very cheap. People are seen dying and no one really cares.

Some years ago my wife and I visited Hong Kong. We had a most enjoyable time in that exciting city. Everything seemed so different from life in Australia. We enjoyed some wonderful tours and saw things and places we never even knew existed.

One of the most exciting trips we had was a one-day trip into China itself. We travelled from Hong Kong to Macau by hydrofoil and soon found ourselves in a bus ready to leave for the border crossing into Communist China. At the border we had to fill in a form stating what we were carrying with us — even the rings on our fingers had to be reported. Guards with rifles entered our bus, collected our forms and then, after our passports had been checked, we crossed the border.

The bus driver spoke excellent English and gave us a commentary of everything we passed. We saw what life in the paddy fields was like. We could see hundreds of ducks in small dams. The countryside was dry and there seemed to be dust everywhere. In many places the road on which we travelled was just a dusty dirt track. But one thing that amazed us all was the number of people walking along the road with huge loads on their shoulders. Others were riding bicycles and these were stacked high with belongings. Most people seemed to be carrying goods as if they were going to a market somewhere.

Here and there we saw groups of people taking a rest from the heat and dust, sitting under trees, talking to each other. Other people just sat beside the road and waved as we passed by.

Suddenly the bus driver called out into his microphone, 'See what's in front of us? We won't be stopping!'

Lying in the middle of the road was a man. He could have been asleep, but I thought that no one would go to sleep in such a dangerous place. Maybe he had collapsed on the road. I thought that he might have been hurt and needed attention. But there were people walking along the road and they just kept walking on without taking any notice of the man on the road. Maybe the man was drunk or even dead! The bus driver wouldn't stop the bus, but simply pulled over to the opposite side of the road and kept on going. He said it was too dangerous to stop in that area.

I still think of that man lying in the middle of that dusty, hot road in Communist China and every time I do I can't help thinking of the story of the Good Samaritan. Maybe someone stopped and helped him — I don't know.

Reader, you and I need mercy from God, because we have offended him by our sinful rebellion. It is as if we have shaken our fist in God's face and said, 'I will live as I please! I will do as I like! I don't want anything to do with you!'

Isn't it wonderful that our God has shown us mercy? Jesus Christ came into this world to die for sinners. If you trust in Jesus Christ as Lord and Saviour, you have really tasted the mercy of God. Your sins have been forgiven and forgotten. You are on your way to heaven to be with Christ for ever.

And because you have tasted God's mercy, your new character will produce a life of mercy towards others. Live your life like the Good Samaritan. And all the good you do, do it in the name of Jesus. In this way he gets the glory and by your actions you may lead someone to faith in your Saviour.

Always remember the words of Jesus: 'Then the King will say to those on his right hand, "Come, you blessed of my Father, inherit the kingdom prepared for you from the foundation of the world: for I was hungry and you gave me food; I was thirsty and you gave me drink; I was a stranger and you took me in; I was naked and you clothed me; I was sick and you visited me; I was in prison and you came to me"... "Assuredly, I say to you, inasmuch as you did it to one of the least of these my brethren, you did it to me"' (Matthew 25:34-36,40).

Activities

● ●

1. Who were the Samaritans?
2. What did Jesus mean when he said that we should be like the 'Good Samaritan'?
3. Why should you help other people?
4. What is 'the golden rule' and what does it teach us? (See Matthew 7:12; Luke 6:31).

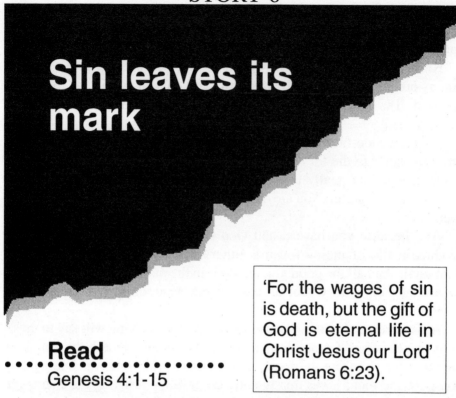

Sin leaves its mark

..... **Read** ....
Genesis 4:1-15

'For the wages of sin is death, but the gift of God is eternal life in Christ Jesus our Lord' (Romans 6:23).

Sin is the most terrible thing in the world. It is disobedience to God's law. And God is angry with sinners.

The Bible has many stories of the sinful behaviour of men and women. We only have to look at our own lives to know that sin is the cause of all unhappiness. And the consequence of sin is death. Today's text tells us plainly, 'The wages of sin is death...' There are two aspects to the death spoken of here. First, there is the death that we see around us every day. It is the death of the body. This death is the wages of sin. There is also a second death spoken of in our text, and that is eternal death, which is the wages paid to all who have not repented of their sins and do not trust in Jesus Christ for their salvation. Sin leaves its mark on each one of us!

My brother and I get on very well together. But when we were young and living on the farm there were times when we upset one another. Occasionally we wouldn't talk to each other for a while, but we always got over it. But one day when we were in the hallway of our home, John ran after me and hit me on the back. He didn't hit me really hard, but he gave me a great fright. In anger I turned around and swung my fist at him. Now that was a terrible thing to do. I should never have raised my hand at my brother. People should never go about hitting one another.

Today's reading is about two brothers, Cain and Abel. These two were the first brothers that the world had known. I'm sure they didn't have many people to talk to. If ever two brothers should have loved one another it should have been Cain and Abel. But the brothers were different to each other in their attitude towards God. Abel was a shepherd who loved God. Cain was a farmer who had no real love for God. The result was that Cain became jealous of Abel and one day murdered him in the field. His jealousy turned to anger, and anger led to hatred, and hatred resulted in the killing of the person he should have loved and protected.

You have read of God's reaction to Cain's terrible deed. Cain's sin left a mark on him. First his heart was filled with fear, for he knew that when others heard of his terrible sin his life would be in danger. But God placed a sign of some kind upon Cain. This sign marked him out as the one who murdered his brother. The sign was also a warning that no one was to kill him. Cain's sin left its mark upon him in a very real way.

Now back to my brother and me in the hallway. I lifted my fist and swung it at John. He simply ducked out of the way and my knuckles smacked into the wall. Then I looked at my fist. The skin from my knuckles was missing and blood was dripping to the floor.

John then said, 'Look at the wall!' When I looked I could see several dents in the wall filled with skin from my knuckles. Both John and I burst out laughing, even though I felt like crying.

Today as I'm typing these words I can still see the scars on my knuckles where I lost my skin on the wall. My sinful action left its mark. And this is the case with all sin. Sin can leave real scars on the body. But other sins cause broken hearts, destroy friendships, upset the conscience, and we could go on and on. However, our text tells us of the greatest scars caused by sin — sickness, tears and death. Every person reading this book will one day die unless the Lord Jesus returns first.

Have you prepared for your death? There is only one way to do so and this too is found in our text: '... but the gift of God is eternal life in Christ Jesus our Lord'. Salvation and eternal life can be yours if you turn from your sinful ways in true repentance and trust in Jesus alone for salvation.

Friend, if you are not a Christian, pray that God will send his Spirit into your heart so you might believe the gospel story and live by faith in Christ, the Son of God.

Activities

●●

1. What are 'the wages of sin'?
2. What is sin?
3. What is God's gift to all who love Jesus?

Thrown out!

Read
Revelation 12:7-12

'So the great dragon was cast out, that serpent of old, called the Devil and Satan, who deceives the whole world; he was cast to the earth, and his angels were cast out with him' (Revelation 12:9).

The book of Revelation is a difficult one to understand, but every Christian should read this book because God has made a wonderful promise to all who read and listen to its words. We read, 'Blessed is he who reads and those who hear the words of this prophecy, and keep those things which are written in it...' (Revelation 1:3).

In the world Christians and the church face great opposition, but the book of Revelation should give every reader great encouragement because in it we are assured that Christ has the victory over all his enemies. Our God reigns and controls the events of history. Satan does not win in the end.

Snakes, or serpents, are mentioned frequently in the Bible. In fact our text for today refers to Satan as 'that serpent of old'. It was Satan who took the form of a snake and tempted Adam and Eve in the Garden of Eden. It was Satan who brought about all the evil in this world's history. Satan is the enemy of God and of humans. We must always be on guard against the temptations of the Evil One.

There have been many times when I have thrown out something, only to find out later that I should have kept it. We have a lovely set of cutlery at

31

home, but it is partly ruined because I wrapped up a fork with the scraps, and tossed it into the rubbish bin, so now we have only five forks to go with the set of six knives. We can't find a replacement fork with the same pattern anywhere. Of course this was an accident and I have been forgiven. And Val and I know that it doesn't really matter, as we still have plenty of forks to use at the meal-table. But there have been times when we have thrown away something that has caused real disappointment later on.

Many years ago, when both of our parents sold their farms, Val and I had the opportunity of keeping some of the equipment that was used in the production of milk. The milk-cans were in really good order, but we decided that we would never need a milk-can. Then there were the cross-cut saws used to cut up firewood. They were always kept in excellent condition, but we decided they would be of no use. And so it was that most of the well-kept equipment used on the farms was either sold or thrown away. The farms were sold and that brought to an end an enjoyable part of our lives.

But today everyone is interested in folk art, and milk-cans and saws have become very valuable. To buy an old battered milk-can costs several hundred dollars. One in new condition just cannot be found anywhere. Val and I searched high and low and eventually found a cross-cut saw, but so far we haven't found a good-quality milk-can. A lady we know has decorated the saw with lovely flowers and the name of our home is painted on it. Many visitors have admired the colourful saw now attached to the brick wall near our front door.

Throwing out once-valuable equipment reminds me of the text and reading for today. Satan was once one of God's glorious angels. But he rebelled against God's rule and was cast out of heaven to earth. There on the earth he tempted Adam and Eve and sin entered the world when they did as Satan suggested. They ate the fruit of the tree of the knowledge of good and evil (read Genesis 2:15-17; 3:1-7).

Today's reading concerns the resurrection and ascension of the Lord Jesus Christ to heaven. When he took his seat upon the throne of God, the salvation of his people was secured. Till then Satan had at times appeared in heaven to make accusations against God and the saints (Job 1:6-12). Before the saving work of Christ, Satan must have said that the saints had no right to be in heaven. But when salvation was accomplished Satan no longer could accuse God of doing the wrong thing by allowing the saints into heaven.

Our reading tells us that there was war in heaven and Satan was cast out. Jesus had finished the work of salvation so there was no reason for Satan to enter heaven at all. He fell to the earth — thrown out like a piece of rubbish. Now Satan spends his time attacking the followers of Christ, tempting them to sin. He also attacks the church, trying to destroy it.

Friend, if you are a Christian, Satan will be at your heels trying to get you to turn away from Christ and so bring shame upon the Saviour. The apostle Peter warns us that 'The devil walks about like a roaring lion, seeking whom he may devour' (1 Peter 5:8). So be on guard! Follow the Lord Jesus carefully and faithfully day by day.

And, reader, if you are not a Christian, Satan has you just where he wants you. You belong to him and he will do all he can to prevent you from turning to Jesus for salvation.

It is my longing that everyone who reads this book comes to saving faith in Christ. Then, and only then, you can rejoice in the words of Jesus when he said that no one can pluck you out of the hands of God (John 10:28-29). God is all-powerful and his people will be safe for ever. When you sin, go to Jesus in prayer and seek forgiveness. And, praise God, your sins will be forgiven. Christians have a wonderful Saviour.

Activities

● ●

1. List four names for the devil.
2. Where would you find the 'tree of the knowledge of good and evil'?
3. What other special tree would Adam and Eve have found nearby?
4. Where in the Bible is Satan called 'a roaring lion'?

What a lovely cake!

Read
....
2 Kings 6:8-17

'The angel of the LORD encamps all around those who fear him, and delivers them' (Psalm 34:7).

We live in a world we can see and touch. When I get out of bed each morning I look through the window and see the new day dawning. When I go outside into the garden I can smell the perfume of the flowers. The sound of birds singing is like music in my ears. I can reach down and pat Wags, my small pet dog who is sitting near my chair. Later I sit at the table, eat my breakfast and really enjoy the lovely taste of food. This is our world. It is real and was created by God through his Son the Lord Jesus Christ.

But my world is not always what it appears to be. One day I thought I saw a letter in the letter-box, but when I had a close look it was just a shadow. I'm sure that there have been many times when your senses have tricked you.

I would like to tell you a story — a true one — about something that was not what it appeared to be. Things happened that people knew nothing about. I can't tell you the real names of the people involved because they would be embarrassed if they read this about themselves. Two people I know very well, a husband and wife — let's call them Jack and Jill — were going to a most important church function. In fact it was the opening of a new church building. They were members of the congregation and were asked to bring along some food for the supper that would follow the opening service. Jack drove the car while Jill carefully balanced the lovely sponge cake on her lap. The sponge had plenty of red, juicy strawberries half buried in the cream carefully spread over the top of the cake.

As the car was about to stop, Jack braked suddenly and the cake slipped from Jill's lap. It was almost on the car floor before she caught it. But the cream and strawberries were all over the place.

'Oh dear!' said Jill. 'Whatever shall we do? The cake is ruined!'

But Jack knew what to do. He said to his wife, 'You just sit there and don't move. I'll fix it up.'

Quickly he raced around to the side of the car where his wife was sitting, and with his hands scooped up the cream and smoothed it over the top of the cake. The cake started to look good again!

'But what about the strawberries?' asked Jill. 'They are covered with cream. You had better throw them away.'

But Jack had the answer to that problem as well. He picked the strawberries out of the cream, smoothed the cream out again and then with his clean handkerchief began to gently wipe the strawberries clean. Finally he replaced them carefully on the cake.

'Now don't say anything,' Jack told Jill. 'No one will ever know what happened.'

Everyone had a wonderful supper and Jill told me she even saw the city mayor eating a slice of her cake. No one realized what had happened. Everything about that cake looked quite normal.

We live in a world where things look normal, but is what we see, hear, smell, touch and taste all there is to this world? The answer is, 'No!' There is an unseen world about us — a world that is as real as the one we can see.

In that world, events of which we have no knowledge are taking place.

Our text tells us that the angel of God is protecting his people. This means that there must be something unseen from which we need to be protected. Satan and the demons are round about us in that unseen world. They are there tempting us to fall into sin. They are there stirring up the hatred of men and women against God's people. That is why the angel of the Lord surrounds the saints. God's angels are there in the unseen world, which is as real as the world in which we live.

In today's Scripture passage we read of an incident in the life of Elisha. The army of the King of Syria was ready to invade the city of Dothan and capture the prophet. When Elisha's servant saw that great army he was very much afraid. But Elisha prayed that God might open the young man's eyes to enable him to see into the unseen world around him. Then Elisha's servant saw the angels of God between the city wall and the invading army. Elisha was saved by God's unseen army.

Many times in the Scriptures we read about the unseen angels of God protecting the saints. In 2 Kings 19 we find the angel of the Lord overthrowing the army of Sennacherib, King of Assyria, when it was about to attack Jerusalem. In one night 185,000 Assyrian soldiers were killed by the angel of the Lord.

Satan is called 'the prince of the power of the air' (Ephesians 2:2). In the unseen world around us a great battle is being fought between the angels of God, who protect the saints, and the demons, led by Satan. Things around us might seem normal, just like that repaired cake, but in the unseen world much is happening and has happened.

Our Saviour Jesus Christ has defeated Satan and the spiritual war is nearly at an end. Soon, when Christ returns, we shall see the angels of God. The unseen world will become our real world and all who love God and live by faith in Christ will enjoy that world for ever.

Reader, do you have a place in the kingdom Christ has prepared for his people? I pray that you will have!

Activities

• •

1. What is a sponge cake?
2. Discuss the events spoken of in 2 Kings 6:8-17. What do they mean for God's people?
3. Who is the king of the demons?

Beware of the chicken!

.... **Read** ....
Deuteronomy 6:1-9

'Train up a child in the way he should go, and when he is old he will not depart from it' (Proverbs 22:6).

Growing up can be a difficult time of life. There is so much to do and to learn. I'm sure that any of my readers who are not still attending school can remember their own schooldays. At school you are taught to read and write. You learn history and geography, how to do mathematics and no doubt younger readers have also been taught how to use a computer.

Mum and Dad are also involved in teaching you how to look after your body. You are taught to brush your teeth, wash behind your ears and comb your hair. No doubt you are also expected to make your bed and keep your room tidy. Growing up is a learning time!

Now today's text teaches us something that is very important. Read the text and think about it for a moment or two. In the text, God reminds us that young people must be taught a right way to live. That way is the way of righteousness — of love towards God and love of all those around us. Everyone is called upon to fear God and trust in Jesus Christ for his or her salvation. Teaching young people the great truths of Scripture is the responsibility of parents. Of course pastors, church leaders, Sunday School teachers and many others help teach young people how to live a life that is pleasing to God. Young people must be taught what is right and what is wrong, what pleases God and what is sinful. And there are times when Mum or Dad will deal out punishment for sinful behaviour.

One day I visited a friend whose family had a lot of chickens and other fowls. They also had four or five dogs. What amazed me was that the dogs kept well away from the fowls. Even the small pups would run away when a chicken came near. I felt sure that at least the pups would have chased the birds, but they showed no interest in them. In fact they seemed frightened of even the smallest chickens. I asked my friend Matthew to explain the reason for the dog fear of the fowls and chickens.

He simply said, 'We trained the dogs when they were pups not to touch a chicken and our training works.'

'Did you smack the pups?' I asked.

The reply was, 'No.' But I noticed a smile on Matthew's face. Then he told me how they taught a young pup to keep away from the fowls.

'There is a lot of work on our farm preparing the chickens for sale. We need dogs, but they must not touch the chickens,' Matthew explained. 'The training is so simple — we put an old feathered chicken skin round a balloon and leave it where the pups play. When they get too close to the make-believe chicken, Dad explodes the balloon. Feathers and dust go everywhere. This doesn't hurt the pups but they get a terrible fright. They simply turn and run to their kennels for safety. When this has happened a few times the pups keep well away from the chickens.'

Parents must train their young children in the ways of the Lord. Young friends, make sure you take notice of those who teach you the things of God, and by God's grace be faithful servants of King Jesus all the days of your life.

Christian parents will always teach their children the ways of God. They will pray for their young ones and will set them an example of godly living. Christian parents want to see their children becoming members of God's family.

Joshua was a great man of God. He loved God and served him faithfully all his life. He taught his family to live the life of faith. One day he said to the Israelites, 'But as for me and my house, we will serve the LORD' (Joshua 24:15). It is my prayer that each of my readers, with their family members, will be able to say the same.

Activities

●●●

a. Who teaches you the right way to live?
b. Why should you obey your parents?
c. Do you think your parents should sometimes smack you if you do not behave?
d. Who was Joshua?

Be prepared!

Read
Luke 12:13-21

'Behold, now is the accepted time; behold, now is the day of salvation' (2 Corinthians 6:2).

When I was a youngster I was a member of the Sea Scouts. With my friends we spent many hours enjoying friendships, learning how to sail and row boats, as well as being encouraged to live an upright life. The motto of the Boy Scouts was, and still is, 'Be prepared!' This is a fine motto to live by and all my life I have tried to be prepared for whatever situation might arise.

I make sure that I have more photocopying paper than I need, just in case I have an urgent need for it. To save making unnecessary trips to town Valerie makes sure we have extra food stored in the pantry. It is wise to 'be prepared' for whatever might happen.

As members of the Sea Scouts we had many very exciting trips in the scout boats. Before anyone could go out in a boat the scoutmaster made sure he could swim. He would take us down to the river-bank — we didn't have a swimming pool in our small town when I was a boy — and there we would swim out to a marker and back. The scoutmaster would swim alongside the lad who was doing the test, just in case anything went wrong.

Most of the boys who joined the Sea Scouts were good swimmers. Even though our town had no swimming pool we lived beside the river and almost every one of my friends could swim. For fun we swam in the river, we fished in the river, we rowed our boats on the river — we loved the water!

Every Sea Scout carried a knife. I don't remember ever using the knife during my scout days — other than to cut up food — but it was there just in case we had to cut a rope if an emergency arose.

In our large boat we carried life-jackets — just in case! We learned how to get a fire going without the use of matches — provided the sun was

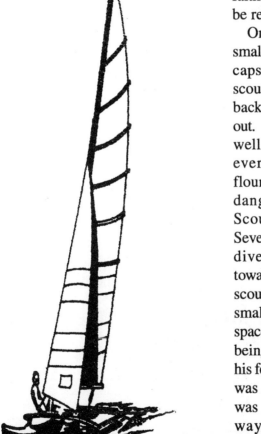

shining! The scout motto was faithfully kept. We were always to be ready for an emergency.

One day as we were sailing our small VJ dinghies one of them capsized. The mast struck one scout across his shoulders and the back of his neck. He was knocked out. At first we thought all was well, but within a few seconds everyone realized the boy floundering in the water was in danger of drowning. But Sea Scouts are always 'prepared'. Several boys from nearby boats dived overboard and swam towards the boy needing help. The scoutmaster was also at hand in a small motor boat. Within a short space of time the injured scout was being supported in the water by his fellow scouts. The scoutmaster was soon on the spot and the boy was in the motor boat and on his way to hospital for an examination.

It wasn't long before the boy was back with us all. He had a bruise across his back, but was well and ready to get into the sailing boat.

The scout motto, 'Be prepared,' was not just a motto. We were all really prepared for whatever might happen, and because of that a life was saved.

Being prepared for what happens in life is the sensible thing to do. And the one event that will happen to every human being — including you, unless the Lord returns beforehand — is that you will die. Have you prepared for this event?

Today's Bible reading is about a man who was not prepared for the day of his death. So unprepared was he that God said of him: 'You fool!'

That rich man had piled up his wealth and was ready to enjoy his retirement, but the days God had allotted him had come to an end. It was time for him to appear before the judgement seat of God. God had no place in his life and now he would find himself eternally in a place where the goodness of God was totally missing. Of what value was his wealth at the moment of death — and the life that followed death?

So, reader, like the Boy Scouts, 'Be prepared!' Be prepared for the day of your death. Go to Jesus even now, just as today's text says, and pray that he might put his Spirit into your heart that you might be enabled to trust in him for your salvation. Ask God to give you the gift of saving faith. Then get on with your life serving Jesus and glorifying him in all you do and say. Then you will be prepared for the day of your death.

Activities

● ●

a. Who are the Sea Scouts?
b. What is the motto of the scouts? What does it mean?
c. How can you prepare for the day of your death?
d. How do you get 'saving faith'?

Do you want a new body in which to live?

'For the trumpet will sound, and the dead will be raised incorruptible, and we shall be changed. For this corruptible must put on incorruption, and this mortal must put on immortality' (1 Corinthians 15:52-53).

When I was the pastor of a church I had four preaching centres and this meant a lot of time driving the car. One of our church members, who was called Stewart, used to drive me to one outlying congregation. It was a long drive, but it gave us plenty of time to talk. For many years we travelled the same road and we were always on the lookout for something new to see.

Just outside one small town there was an old house. Children could always be seen playing around as we drove past. The house had a rusty tin roof, the walls were in need of painting and the grass around the house was usually quite long. One of the stands for the water tank had collapsed and the tank was lying on its side. In fact when Stewart and I drove past the house we would often comment on the sad state of the building and wonder how long it would be before it all fell down.

Still it was home to a family who lived there and I feel sure they were happy. Many times in winter we would see the smoke curling up from the chimney. It would have been nice and warm inside. But outside, the building was falling apart.

One Sunday as we drove past we noticed that work had started on a new house. Piles of bricks were to be seen and building timber was spread about. Over several months we saw the changes in the building. The new house was built on a cement block and gradually the brick walls could be seen rising around the wooden framework. Then the tiled roof was added and the new house was well on its way to completion.

We saw the children playing around their new home. The old home was about to be left for the new one. Several months later the old house was deserted and we could see smoke curling up from the chimney of the new one. Over the weeks a garden appeared, the lawn was mown and shrubs could be seen in the garden. The old house seemed to go to rack and ruin very quickly. No one lived in it and one day we noticed that several windows were broken. Cows also wandered about in what had been the front garden. Now when you drive past that area the old house has gone. It must have been knocked down — or have fallen down — and all of the building materials removed.

Now our bodies are like that old house. As young people we have fresh, new bodies, but over the years the home in which we live begins to wear out. I look at myself and see the bald patches where I used to have hair. I take out my teeth to clean them and need glasses to find my toothbrush. My body is getting old. It is like that old house — it is beginning to fall apart. But I still feel young. It's just my body that is wearing out.

An old man once said, 'They say I am growing old because my hair is silvered, and there are crow's feet on my forehead, and my step is not as firm and elastic as before. But they are mistaken; that is not me. The knees are weak, but the knees are not me. The brow is wrinkled, but the brow is not me. This is the house I live in: but I am young — younger than I was ever before.' [1] The day is coming when my body will wear out completely and my heart will stop beating. I shall die. My body will be buried in the cemetery and over time it will return to the dust. But the real me will still be alive. My soul will be with Christ in heaven and that is not the end.

When Jesus returns to this earth my soul will be reunited with a new body. The resurrection will take place and I shall have a brand-new body that will never wear out. In that new body I shall live for ever in the new creation that God has prepared for all who love Jesus.

Christ came into this world to save his people — both body and soul! And as surely as Jesus rose from the grave so also all will rise again. The saints will rise in glorious new bodies. But those who have no interest in Christ will rise in bodies of shame.

Friend, what do you have to look forward to when the Lord Jesus returns? Wouldn't it be wonderful to know that a new Christlike body will be yours when the Saviour returns? This will be so if you are trusting in Christ alone for your salvation.

Activities

● ●

1. Discuss some of the events that will take place when Jesus Christ returns to earth.
2. What is meant by 'incorruption'?
3. Why are our bodies wearing out?
4. What are some of the signs that our bodies are wearing out?

1. Henry Durbanville, *The Best Is Yet To Be,* B. McCall Barbour, Scotland, 1972, p.12.

Security in Jesus

Read
John 10:22-30

'All that the Father gives me will come to me, and the one who comes to me I will by no means cast out' (John 6:37).

We live in a frightening world. Every day we hear in the news about murders, thefts, or young people being abused, and on TV we see men and women being killed in wars in various parts of our world. In some areas it is not safe to go out after dark. Indeed, in some places it is not safe even to go out during the daylight hours. People want to feel secure, so we have police who do what they can to catch those who make life a misery for so many.

Twice our home has been broken into and now we have security bars on some windows. But even so we don't feel totally secure. In fact I don't believe that anyone can reach a state where he or she can say, 'I am totally secure. No one can cause me or my family any harm.'

Some years ago my wife and I had a holiday in Thailand and Malaysia. We had friends in the Australian Air Force who were living in Penang. They invited us to fly over and spend some time with them. This we did, but we added Thailand to our trip.

Now in that part of the world drugs are a problem. There are signs everywhere warning travellers that if they are caught with drugs in their possession they could face the death sentence. My wife Valerie was very concerned about the possibility of someone secretly placing drugs in our luggage in order to smuggle them somewhere without risk to themselves.

So our suitcases had good steel locks on them. I thought they were very secure, but Valerie was always uneasy when we had to hand them over to others. She had the feeling that someone might still be able to put drugs in our luggage. There was no real security.

When we entered Malaysia from Thailand our bags were thoroughly searched. The people working at the immigration section of the airport made us unlock our suitcases and then they closely examined everything. After a very close search we were allowed to enter Malaysia. All round us were large signs warning travellers of the penalties if they were caught with drugs in their possession.

In Malaysia we had a wonderful time. We visited places we had only ever read about. There were temples everywhere and we have some great photographs of the places we visited.

When the time came to leave our friends, Valerie carefully packed our suitcases and locked them securely. No one was going to hide drugs in our luggage! Upon our reaching the airport the customs officer who took our suitcases asked for the keys and unlocked them. They wanted once again to make a thorough search of our possessions to

make sure we were not carrying drugs. As we had to change planes, both Valerie and I were still concerned that someone could tamper with our bags and hide drugs in them. We both felt insecure about the situation. But we need not have worried at all for as soon as our bags had been searched, the locks were put in place and then one of the men took out strips of very strong nylon which a machine wrapped very tightly around our suitcases. There were three or four strips about each piece of luggage. The strips were sealed together and it was then impossible for anyone to tamper with our luggage.

At long last Valerie felt secure. She was now sure that no one could hide anything in our suitcases. In fact when we reached Sydney Airport the immigration officials didn't even bother looking into our sealed bags. They were X-rayed, but no one checked for drugs. Our luggage had been securely locked.

In this world there is little security anywhere. However, if we are Christians we have perfect spiritual security in Jesus. Our text tells us that all who go to Christ for salvation will be received. None will be turned away. And the reading for today drives this wonderful truth home to our hearts. Jesus tells his people that they belong to him, have eternal life and 'they shall never perish' (John 10:28).

There is security in Jesus. No one can snatch us out of the hands of our Saviour. He will never let us go. If my salvation depended upon my hanging onto Jesus, I would never be saved. I am weak but he is strong and can protect me from all the dangers that Satan throws at me.

The apostle Paul asked the question: 'Who shall separate us from the love of Christ?' (Romans 8:35). He answered his own question by telling us that nothing in this world, or the unseen world — not even death — can separate us from the love of God which is found in Jesus Christ.

This world is a very insecure place, but when you belong to Christ your salvation is most secure. We have the promise of Christ concerning his people: 'Neither shall anyone snatch them out of my hand' (John 10:28).

Friends, our Christ has all power in heaven and earth. One day every one of his people will reach that heavenly shore. This world is most insecure, but there is security in Jesus Christ. May you be one of those who are secure in the love of God as found in Jesus Christ.

Activities

● ●

1. What people go to Jesus for salvation?
2. Why is it impossible for God's people to be lost?
3. What does Satan do in his efforts to prevent people from becoming followers of Christ?

No crosses allowed here!

Read

Hebrews 11:23-40

'If the world hates you, you know that it hated me before it hated you' (John 15:18).

Jesus told the people of his day that the great commandment was: '"You shall love the Lord your God with all your heart, with all your soul, and with all your mind." This is the first and great commandment. And the second is like it: "You shall love your neighbour as yourself." On these two commandments hang all the Law and the Prophets' (Matthew 22:37-40). And this is how it should be, for we are told that 'God is love' (1 John 4:8).

Christians are called upon to love all, even their enemies. We are to do good to everyone and never become involved in activities that will cause hurt. Christians should always remember the story of the Good Samaritan and the words of Christ following that parable. He said, 'Go and do likewise' (Luke 10:37).

When Christians meet other Christians there should always be a real joy in their hearts for they are meeting brothers and sisters who are members of God's family. Together they make up the living church — all saved by Christ, the sin-bearer, all the dwelling-place of the Holy Spirit, and all on their way to live eternally with Christ in the new heavens and the new earth. Christians have so much in common. How they should love one another!

But Satan does all he can to cause non-Christians to hate the followers of Christ. Jesus warned all who would follow him that this would happen.

In today's text Jesus said to his followers, 'If the world hates you, you know that it hated me before it hated you.'

Down through the ages Christians have been hounded throughout the world. They were thrown into the Roman arena to be torn to pieces by wild animals. Many have been burned at the stake and treated in the most horrible ways by people who hate Christ and the wonderful salvation found in him. Even today we read about Christians in various parts of the world being killed, or locked up in prison, for the simple reason that they love and worship Jesus Christ.

Some time ago, as I mentioned in the previous story, my wife and I visited Malaysia. We had a lovely time in Penang. The shopping was very exciting as bargaining was done everywhere. The people were very polite and kind to us and we enjoyed our stay. But the situation there as far as Christians are concerned is not good. They are allowed to meet for worship, but there are very strict warnings that Muslims are not to be approached with the good news concerning Christ. So many in that land have no time for Christianity, and indeed hate the Christian religion. I have a news-sheet from one Christian church and on the bottom of the page it states: 'For Non-Muslims only'. If these words had not been included the local congregation would have been in trouble with the authorities.

When I paid for a pair of shoes that I purchased during the trip I found that I had in my hand, amongst other money, two Malaysian $5 notes. I was looking closely at the notes while the salesman was putting my new shoes in a bag, and I noticed a difference between them. I thought to myself, 'This is unusual. I think I might have found a rare $5 note.'

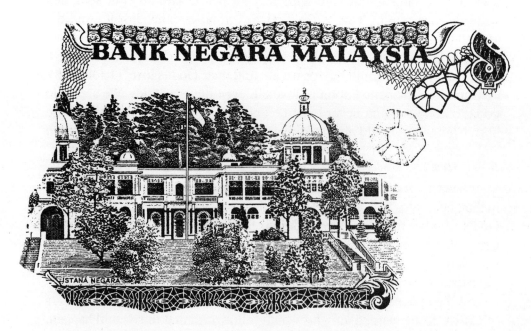

I quickly put the two notes back into my wallet and still have them in my possession. When I arrived where we were staying I showed the notes to my friend and said, 'Look at this! These notes are different. I think I might have a $5 note that is rare.' Then I pointed to the picture of the palace found on one side of the note. It looked an impressive building. In front of the building there was a flag-pole, but it was not the same on each note. On one note the flag-pole had a crossbar near the top, whilst on the other it was simply an upright pole, with no crossbar.

My friend Peter looked at the two notes and then said, 'No, you haven't found a rare note at all. What happened was this. Look at the flag-pole with the crossbar — what does it remind you of?'

'It looks like a cross,' I replied.

'That's right,' said Peter. 'Some local religious groups complained that the symbol of Christianity had no place on a Malaysian $5 note. The government agreed and now the flag-pole is just a pole.'

Isn't this a sad situation? Christianity is hated so much in parts of the world that governments would try to get rid of everything that could remind people of the Christian church. This is the truth that is taught in Psalm 2:1-3:

Why do the nations rage,
And the people plot a vain thing?
The kings of the earth set themselves,
And the rulers take counsel together,
Against the LORD and against his Anointed, saying,
'Let us break their bonds in pieces
And cast away their cords from us.'

The cry of the godless is: 'We will not have this man to reign over us!' (Luke 19:14). They hate the Christian religion and if they had their way they would destroy the church from the face of the earth.

But our God rules this earth and we have Christ's promise that even the gates of hell — in other words, Satan himself — cannot destroy the church (Matthew 16:18). Brothers and sisters in Christ, we have the victory through Jesus Christ our Lord, just as the great saints spoken of in today's Bible reading did.

Activities

●●●

1. What is 'the first and great commandment'? Learn Matthew 22:37-40 by heart.
2. Discuss the reasons for the crucifixion of Christ.
3. Why do people object to having Christ rule over them?
4. Why should we read our Bibles?

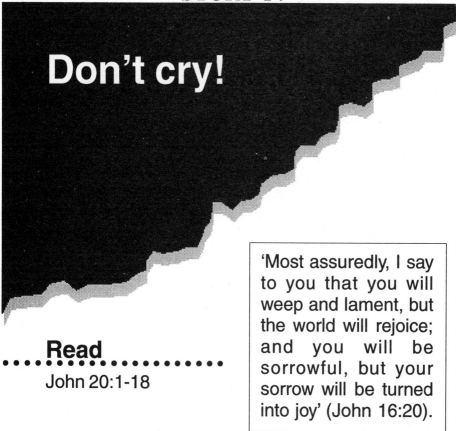

Don't cry!

Read

John 20:1-18

'Most assuredly, I say to you that you will weep and lament, but the world will rejoice; and you will be sorrowful, but your sorrow will be turned into joy' (John 16:20).

Sunday, or the Lord's Day, is a wonderful day. For the Christian it should be the best day of the week, because it reminds us of the resurrection of our Saviour, the Lord Jesus Christ. Christ rose from the dead and stepped out of the tomb on the first day of the week. Sunday is the day when Christians meet with one another to worship God and give thanks for their salvation in Jesus Christ.

But can you imagine how the friends of Jesus must have felt when they saw him die upon the cross? Our text tells us how they felt: they wept and lamented about what had happened to Jesus.

Now I'm sure there have been times when you have been unhappy and cried. I can remember a time when two of my grandchildren were most upset. Jessica and Scott had pet rabbits which they had reared from the day they were born. The mother had refused to feed them, so Scott and Jessica decided to try to feed the tiny little babies themselves, using an eye-dropper to give them milk. With the help of their mum and dad the babies survived.

The two young rabbits were so tame, I think they thought that Jessica and Scott were their mothers. They lived in a cage in the garden, but were let out to run around. They ate the lettuce plants and even tried to eat the

tomatoes. Jessica and Scott never shouted at them for doing the wrong thing. They loved them greatly. In fact the rabbits were allowed inside the house. They would always run to the children when they were called.

But one day we had a phone call. It was Scott, who through tears said he had some very sad news. And sad it was! A dog had jumped over the fence during the night and killed both pet rabbits.

Jessica and Scott were heartbroken. They must have felt in some small way what the disciples and friends of Jesus felt when they saw him crucified and dying upon the cross. Those cruel men and women who hated Jesus rejoiced to see him die. But tears must have flowed down the faces of those who loved Jesus as they saw him die in such a horrible way.

Now in Psalm 30:5 we read some wonderful words: 'Weeping may endure for a night, but joy comes in the morning.' It is a glorious truth that our life is not all sadness, but after sadness comes joy. Sometimes we think we shall never be happy again, but as the time goes by happiness returns.

Scott and Jessica wept many tears for their pet rabbits, but their dad took them to town the next day where in a pet shop they saw two small white rabbits about six weeks old. They weren't sure at first if they wanted the new rabbits, but a day later a car drove into our driveway and two smiling grandchildren hopped out, each with a lovely albino rabbit. They cuddled their new rabbits and introduced them to us as Snowflake and Lilywhite. There were no more tears!

Now think of the disciples and others who saw Jesus crucified. How they wept! But three days later their weeping gave way to joy, as they

learned that Christ had conquered death. He stepped out of that tomb in a new resurrected body. When Christ's friends met him again at first they couldn't believe their eyes. But there was Jesus — he was alive! Now the tears were gone. Their sorrow was turned into joy!

Reader, if you are a Christian you have reason for sorrow. Your sins nailed Jesus to that terrible cross. But there should also be a real joy in your heart, for Jesus has dealt with your sins. God has forgiven you for the sake of Jesus.

And the best is yet to come, for one day we shall see Jesus, our Saviour, face to face and enjoy him for ever. There will be no more sin, no more tears — just everlasting joy in the presence of Christ.

Activities

● ●

1. What makes Sunday a special day to the Christian?
2. How should you spend the Lord's Day?
3. Some people call the Lord's Day 'the Sabbath'. What does Sabbath mean?

Watch out for the soap!

Read
Matthew 13:24-30, 36-43

'When the Son of Man comes in his glory, and all the holy angels with him, then he will sit on the throne of his glory. All the nations will be gathered before him, and he will separate them one from another, as a shepherd divides his sheep from the goats' (Matthew 25:31-32).

'Don't get caught buying cheap imitations,' I was told before Valerie and I, and two of our daughters, boarded the plane for a holiday in Hong Kong. When we arrived there and wandered through the shopping areas we found many wonderful things for sale. We saw what appeared to be really good-quality clothing and many garments were labelled with very well-known brand names. But they were so cheap we knew something was wrong. When we picked up the clothes and looked at them closely, we could tell they were not the real thing.

Of course, there were shopping centres where genuine good-quality clothes could be purchased and they were not very cheap. But from a distance it was difficult to tell which was the genuine article and which was the fake.

In the church today we find that most people profess to be Christians. They claim that they love Christ and are saved by his death upon the cross at Calvary. But we must ask, 'Are they the real thing?' An even more important question to which each of us needs to know the answer is: 'Am I a Christian, or just a hypocrite?'

Jesus spoke some very serious words that I want you to think about. He said one day, 'Not everyone who says to me, "Lord, Lord," shall enter the kingdom of heaven, but he who does the will of my Father in heaven' (Matthew 7:21). In other words, Jesus warns us all that on the Day of Judgement there will be many disappointed people who professed to be his followers and thought their profession of faith to be a true one, but it was not. That is why everyone who claims to be a Christian should make sure they really do have a saving faith in the Son of God. So often the Christian and the hypocrite look just alike. It is hard to tell the difference.

Today's reading is the parable Christ told about the wheat and the tares. While the wheat and the tares grew together in the field, it was almost impossible to distinguish the weeds from the wheat. Jesus was telling his hearers that sometimes you cannot tell if a person is a Christian or not.

Many years ago I was sent to teach at a small school in the country. It was a lovely area and the people were very kind to us. I became a good friend of the man who was the president of the Parents' and Citizens' Association. One afternoon we invited him and his wife home for afternoon tea. I decided to play a trick on him and asked my wife if we had some Sunlight soap. Now Sunlight soap is the colour of cheese. I carefully grated some of the soap onto several biscuits. Val had prepared some biscuits with genuine cheese on them, but it was almost impossible to tell which was which.

When our new friends arrived, we sat down and talked about school. Soon a cup of tea was on the table and I watched as Jim took a biscuit from the plate offered to him. He picked up a biscuit covered with the grated soap. To Jim the cheese looked like the real thing. It was only after he had put the biscuit and 'cheese' into his mouth and began to chew that he noticed the difference. A strange look came over his face and he asked, 'What have you done? This cheese tastes terrible!'

Of course, he washed the terrible taste out of his mouth and he said, 'Watch out! One day I'll get you back!'

Jim could tell the difference between the cheese and the soap only when he put it in his mouth and tasted.

In our parable Jesus warns us that in the church there will be a mixture of those who are truly born again and others who do not really know Christ as their Lord and Saviour. This means we need to be very careful in our dealings with the people who make up our congregation. We must show love to them all — even those who fall into terrible sin, as Peter did when he denied that he knew Christ. Always remember that Peter repented of his sin and went on to serve Christ faithfully for many years until his death.

We need to be very careful in making judgements about other professing Christians. It could well be that someone we think is a weed is a Christian of little faith — but still one loved by Christ and saved by his precious blood.

The Lord, in his parable, has taught that the wheat and the tares were to be left growing together. At the harvest-time the person doing the harvesting would be able to tell which was the wheat and which was the tare. Then the tares could be cut down, bundled up and thrown into the fire. God knows who are his people. It is God who will judge the people of this world, through his Son Jesus Christ.

Of course, there are times when the church must put members out of the fellowship because, by their words and their lives, they show their profession of faith to be false. But the church must be so careful in dealing with those who claim to love Christ and live outwardly moral lives. We are to treat all who profess faith in Christ as our brothers and sisters in Christ.

The questions we all need to ask ourselves are these: 'Am I a Christian? Is it possible that I will hear Christ's words: "I never knew you... Depart from me..."?' Look at yourself and the life you are living. Do you love God? Do you love the people about you — even your enemies? Do you, with God's help, try to obey his commandments, because you love Jesus who said, 'If you love me, keep my commandments'? (John 14:15). When you fall into sin do you confess your sin to God and ask for forgiveness? And do you see evidence of the fruit of the Spirit in your life? Read and think about the words of the apostle Paul: 'But the fruit of the Spirit is love, joy, peace, longsuffering, kindness, goodness, faithfulness, gentleness, self-control' (Galatians 5:22-23). Ask yourself, 'Do these words describe the kind of person I am?'

You will never be perfect in this life, but if you have been born again you will be able to see the evidence of a true Christian faith. May God be pleased to bless you with a genuine faith in Jesus Christ.

Activities

■■

1. In the text, who is represented by the goats?
2. How can you tell if a person is a Christian?
3. What terrible sin did Peter commit?
4. Discuss the fruit of the Spirit.

Obey your parents

Read
....
1 Samuel 2:12-17,
23-25

'Children, obey your parents in the Lord, for this is right. "Honour your father and mother," which is the first commandment with promise: "that it may be well with you and you may live long on the earth"' (Ephesians 6:1-3).

Life on the farm was in some ways lonely. Our friends lived next door, but next door was a kilometre (just over half a mile) or so away. There were always plenty of jobs to be done, so when my brother and I had the opportunity to go to  town we usually took it. Then there were those special occasions when, with our friends, we went to the nearby town to see a film at the cinema. In those days it was safe to walk the streets, even late at night. John and I, with our mates, would ride our bicycles to the town, have a pleasant time at the pictures and be home by ten o'clock.

However, there were times when Dad would say, 'No, not tonight. There is work to be done this afternoon and you'll be too worn out to go anywhere.' Of course, John and I were never happy to hear these words and sometimes complained to Dad about his decision. The young folk on nearby farms met with the same refusals from their parents, and I know they complained too. But we knew our parents were to be obeyed and we did as we were told — even though at times we thought Dad was hard on us.

Our text tells us that we are to obey our parents in all things — unless, of course, they tell us to do something that is against the law of God. Then, and then only, may we refuse to obey. God promises blessings to children who obey their parents and every child needs to read the words of the text and pay attention to it. You must think God's promises through and pray that God will give you the grace to obey and respect your mum and dad.

One Saturday a young lad whom I know very well wanted to go to the pictures with his friends. They had made arrangements the day before to meet and during Saturday afternoon young Peter asked his father if he could go to see the film with his friends. But Dad had other plans. That afternoon Dad had several workmen in the barn as it was hay-making time. Peter's help was needed so Dad said, 'I'm sorry, but not this Saturday. You can go next Saturday. Today I need your help here.'

To say the least, Peter was not happy with his dad's decision. During the afternoon he kept complaining to his father: 'Dad, I want to go. You never let me go to the pictures. All my mates will be there and I never get a chance to go with them!'

Of course, this was not true. Peter went to the pictures many times, but on that particular Saturday his help was needed. Peter knew this, but for hours he complained to his father. I know the workmen who were in the barn didn't help the situation, but kept saying to Peter, 'Keep asking, Peter. If you complain enough, your dad will give in and let you go.' And so the complaints continued all afternoon.

When Peter saw some of his friends riding their bikes along the road he threw down the bundle of wire he was carrying and shouted to his father, 'I'm going to the pictures and you can't stop me!'

Peter turned and ran for the house which was about 300 metres from the barn. The workmen saw what was happening and began to cheer him on. Peter's father, however, was not going to let his son get away with disobedience. He dropped the tools in his hands and set off in pursuit of Peter. As he ran he began to unbuckle the belt which held up his trousers.

The men in the barn shouted out, 'Run, Peter! Run!' But Dad was gaining on Peter. Then as he took off his belt, his trousers started falling down. A roar of laughter went up from the workmen as Peter's father tripped on his fallen trousers and fell over in the long grass.

Peter stopped running and looked around at his father. He knew he had done wrong. He knew he was in trouble. Dad was embarrassed and it was his fault. Peter slowly began to walk back towards his dad who was struggling to his feet as he pulled up his trousers. Brushing the grass from his clothes, he began to buckle up his belt.

As Peter came up to his father he said, 'I'm sorry, Dad. I should have obeyed you. I know I can go to the pictures next Saturday. Let's go back and get on with the work.'

His father looked at him and then a smile began to spread over his face. Even so, Peter knew his dad was very serious when he said, 'Don't you ever try that again. You made a fool of me in front of the men. You deserve a good hiding, young man.' Then he pointed to the barn and continued, 'Let's get back to work. The sooner we're finished, the sooner you can get to bed.'

Today's Bible reading is about the wicked sons of the prophet Eli. Their father warned them about their wicked behaviour, but we read, 'Nevertheless they did not heed the voice of their father...' (v. 25). Because of their wickedness these young men were punished by God — they were killed in battle.

Let us all show respect to our parents, that God's promise concerning obedience may be ours.

Activities

1. What is meant by 'Honour your father and mother'?
2. What was the cause of the death of Eli's sons?
3. How did Eli fail his sons?
4. Besides your parents, who else should you respect?

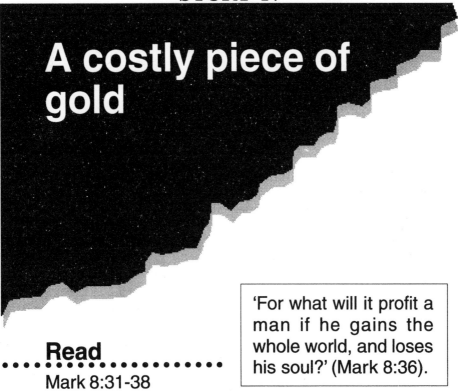

A costly piece of gold

....**Read**.............
Mark 8:31-38

'For what will it profit a man if he gains the whole world, and loses his soul?' (Mark 8:36).

This chapter was contributed by my brother, Rev. John Cromarty. It was first published as an article in *The Geelong Advertiser* following the visit of Professor Douglas MacMillan to Geelong, Victoria, Australia, where John is a minister. The article is reproduced here, in a slightly edited form, with permission.

A few years ago we had a distinguished visitor in our home. His name was Douglas MacMillan. In his youth he tossed the caber and wrestled at the Highland Games in Scotland. He was also a shepherd. In his early twenties he came to see his need of a Saviour, and with a broken heart because of his sins against God, he put his trust in the Lord Jesus Christ and thus commenced a totally new life. He entered the gospel ministry and later became a professor at a theological college in Edinburgh.

A few months after undergoing serious heart surgery, and back once again in the pastoral ministry, Douglas went for his usual evening stroll, but did not return. After a brief search, his body was found slumped beside a pathway not far from his home.

When this news reached me I was very sad indeed. He was a man in his mid-fifties. He was such a good man and he bore a powerful Christian testimony. He was in great demand as a preacher and teacher. He had written a number of very fine Christian books. *The Lord our Shepherd* is a gem — a shepherd writing about the Shepherd! And now this shepherd is experiencing the fulness of joy in the fellowship of his Saviour, the Good Shepherd!

To most people, Douglas could have achieved almost anything in life — in sport, in teaching, academically. But he chose Christ. His values and outlook were moulded by a view of eternity. He saw that everything was empty and all was lost if he did not live to please his Lord and Saviour, who said, 'What profit is there if a man gains the whole world and loses his own soul?' (Mark 8:36). Douglas is now with Christ whom he so earnestly loved and served, and his peace and joy are unending.

When Douglas was in Geelong, he told me of his maternal grandfather who had come to Australia during the gold-rushes, but who had been killed at Ballarat in a mine-shaft accident. His family had no more information.

I began a search at Ballarat Library, then Melbourne and finally in the historical archives at Laverton and was able to discover the details (including a surgeon's report) that had eluded the family since 1852.

Angus MacDonald and his two friends, James Henderson and Duncan McDugall, had arrived in the colony in early 1852 and were working a claim at Eureka in Ballarat. On 2 November 1852 there was a fall of earth in the tunnel where Angus was digging.

Part of the sworn testimony of one of his mates is as follows: 'I heard the deceased cry out: 'Duncan, bear a hand and pick some of this stuff off me ... or I'll be smothered!' In about two minutes I heard his groans. I called to him several times but got no answer... I went for the doctor... It was about twenty-five minutes from the time the hole fell in till they dug him out. When he was brought out of the hole he was quite dead. The deceased and I were shipmates. I have been in this colony about seven months.'

Angus MacDonald had come in search of gold. He had found some. A few ounces were sent back to his wife and child in Scotland. When Angus died, he was in his early twenties. I do not know if Angus was a Christian. He was out here seeking earthly treasures. Had he heeded Jesus' words to 'Seek first the kingdom of God'? Had he found the heavenly treasure through Jesus Christ?

I would be the last person to pass judgement on him for seeking that precious yellow metal! But had he sought and entered the kingdom of God through a personal faith in Jesus Christ as Saviour? Was the Lord precious to him? That was all that mattered now.

And after all, that is the ultimate question, for as I have mentioned earlier, Jesus said, 'What profit is there if a man gains the whole world and loses his own soul?' (Mark 8:36).

And I put these questions to you today: Of what worth is your eternal salvation and security? What price do you place on heaven? For what do you live? What are your priorities — earthly or heavenly? The temporary or the enduring? Is your treasure found in this world or in heaven?

A Scottish preacher who lived at the same time that Angus MacDonald was in Scotland wrote these words:

I heard the voice of Jesus say,
'Come unto me and rest.
Lay down thou weary one, lay down
Thy head upon my breast.'
I came to Jesus as I was,
Weary and worn and sad.
I found in him a resting-place,
And he has made me glad.

It will be to your eternal profit if you can say this too. Otherwise all is loss!

Activities

●●●

1. What are the 'Highland Games'?
2. Who is the Christian's Shepherd?
3. What is the most valuable part of you?
4. What is the most important thing anyone can do during his or her lifetime?

Beware of the dog!

Read
Isaiah 40:10-24

'Behold, the Lord GOD shall come with a strong hand, and his arm shall rule for him; behold, his reward is with him, and his work before him' (Isaiah 40:10).

If someone asked you to repeat the words of John 3:16 I'm sure you would be able to do so. It is the best-known and best-loved text in the Bible. It tells us of God's great love for this world of sinners. God loved his creation so dearly that he sent his only Son into the world to die for a people whom he would save. The best-loved psalm is Psalm 23. This psalm is about God the Shepherd, who cares for his sheep.

It seems that every Christian has a favourite section of the Bible. One small portion of the Scriptures that I particularly love is the passage found in today's reading. Before you read this story, look at verses 10 and 11 of Isaiah 40 and think hard about them. When you have done that read on.

Most children have pets at some time in their lives. My brother John and I had many pets on the farm, and dogs were always amongst the ones we loved best. They would follow us everywhere.

But there was one dog I remember very well. We called him Butch. He was a good friend to John and me — always at our side when we walked about the farm. He tried to follow us to school and when we went fishing he would come and sit beside us for hours. He loved eating the cooked prawns which we used for bait.

Butch was tough and brave. He didn't seem to be scared of anything. He would round up the cows and if they didn't move fast enough for him he would bite their heels. When they kicked out at him he would duck down and then bite again. Sometimes he would be kicked by a bad-tempered cow, but back he would go again to round them up. When it came to facing the bull he was very brave. Sometimes the bull would turn around and face him. The angry bull would toss dirt up in the air and shake his horns. But Butch would put his head down and run at the bull, barking and snapping at him, and it wouldn't be long before the bull turned and ran where Butch wanted him to go.

Butch was a great dog — strong and courageous. If strangers came around the house, he would start to bark and snarl. We thought he might tear someone's legs off if he really became angry. Butch was a good watchdog. He was afraid of nothing. But Butch was also a big softie. He would rub against our legs and put his head up so we could pat him. He would lick our legs and jump all over us wanting to play.

We also had a cat. Now dogs and cats don't usually get on well with one another, but Butch would find Tess the cat and together they would eat a meal. Sometimes we would find Butch sound asleep and there would be Tess lying between his legs. It was hard to believe that ferocious Butch was so kind to Tess.

There were two sides to the character of Butch. He was a strong, courageous dog, frightened of nothing, but he was also a kind, loving dog. When Tess had kittens it was Butch who used to go over and lick them.

Today's Bible passage is about the character of God. First of all, we know our God is all-powerful. He is the one who created the world and who controls its history. Our God is the almighty ruler of the universe. How we should stand back in holy fear of God!

But in verse 11 of our reading we find something different in the character of God. Our strong, all-powerful, holy God is also a gentle God. Think

about our majestic God who rules all things and hates sin. How wonderful and reassuring it is to read the words:

> He will feed his flock like a shepherd;
> He will gather the lambs with his arm,
> And carry them in his bosom,
> And gently lead those who are with young.

Our great God deals with us as a loving shepherd looks after the sheep. If you belong to Jesus, you can call God 'Father'. This is a wonderful privilege. It is our God who has saved his people through the work of his only Son, the Lord Jesus Christ. It is our God who one day will give us the new heavens and the new earth to be our home for ever. And he will always care for us as a good Shepherd watching over his sheep.

Activities

• •

1. Discuss Psalm 23. Now learn the psalm by heart.
2. Why may Christians call God 'Father'?
3. Who are Christ's sheep?

Where's your bed?

...... **Read** ....
Matthew 8:14-22

'Foxes have holes and birds of the air have nests, but the Son of Man has nowhere to lay his head' (Matthew 8:20).

What type of bed do you sleep in? I imagine it is a reasonably soft bed that is comfortable for a good night's rest. My wife and I have a queen-sized bed, with a firm mattress. Attached to the ceiling over the bed we have an electric fan. This is great in summertime. During winter we use a small electric heating pad. Our bed is very comfortable. We didn't buy the first bed we saw, but looked around till we found the one that suited us best. We spend about a third of our lives in bed, so it is important to have a bed in which we can sleep comfortably.

But there are people today who have no homes and find it necessary to sleep on concrete paths, on grass under bridges — anywhere they can lay down their head. I'm sure these people don't sleep so well. Their beds are not comfortable and the places where they sleep are probably not very safe. Many, I'm sure, would go to sleep with one eye open. It is a tragedy to read of people who have no home to call their own and we who have so much should always be ready to help those in need.

Our text for today reminds us that Jesus had no permanent home when he began preaching and teaching. He was always moving from place to place with his disciples and probably they could never be sure where they would spend the night. I can well imagine that some nights were spent outdoors in the cold weather. At times life was very difficult for Jesus and his disciples as they went about preaching the good news to the people of Israel.

Some time ago my brother and I went fishing. We planned a trip out to sea and decided we would spend a night on a small island at the mouth of the river. Our hope was to catch some good bream during the night. Then as soon as the sky began to grow light in the rising sun we would cross the bar (the shallow stretch of water at the point where the river enters the ocean) and be out to sea searching for the really big fish. We carried plenty of food with us as well as an old blanket each to throw over us during the night. But when you find yourself on a sandy beach with water in front of you and a cold wind blowing in your face life becomes very unpleasant.

We caught a few fish early in the night and then found the time dragging. 'Let's try sleeping,' John suggested. Of course I was in full agreement, but then the trouble began. Sand is cold and hard to rest on. We didn't have

pillows, so we made them out of piles of sand. But the sand was not as comfortable as our beds. Our sand-pillows were hard and cold. Then the mosquitoes began to bite. Our blankets weren't keeping us warm, so John suggested we light a fire for warmth. We also hoped the smoke from the fire would drive away the mosquitoes.

Soon we had a blazing fire going and thought we could settle down for a night's rest. However, the smoke stung our eyes and we found that while we got too hot on the side that was nearest the fire our other side was freezing cold. Then we decided to light a second fire and sleep between the two. Between the smoke, the hard sand, the heat from the fire and the cool breeze that was blowing, we found it almost impossible to sleep. Eventually the sky began to lighten and we headed out to sea where we caught some quite big snapper.

That night John and I had nowhere to lay our heads in comfort. We found life hard and decided that in future if we ever wanted to spend a night on the island we would come better prepared. But after the day's fishing we arrived home to a warm shower, a hot meal and then our lovely, soft beds.

Jesus suffered greatly for his people. When he came into this world he did so as a real man. He knew what it was to be without a bed and to go hungry. Although he was the one through whom the universe was created, Jesus had no permanent home. He had 'nowhere to lay his head'. It does us all the world of good to think about the suffering of our Saviour Jesus Christ. He suffered greatly before his crucifixion. The cross was the climax of his sufferings for his people.

If you are a Christian then show your love for Jesus by obedience to his commands. Thank him again and again for all that he has done for you.

If you are not a Christian, then ask Christ to send the Holy Spirit into your heart so that you might see your sins and your need of a Saviour. May God be pleased to bless all who read these words.

Activities

• •

1. Where did Jesus sleep each night?
2. Can you name one person in whose home Jesus stayed during his preaching ministry?
3. What home has Jesus prepared for his people?

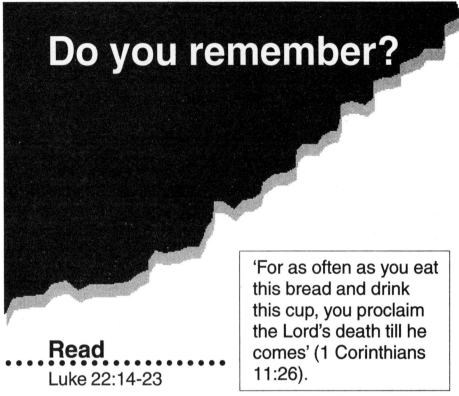

Do you remember?

.... **Read** ....
Luke 22:14-23

'For as often as you eat this bread and drink this cup, you proclaim the Lord's death till he comes' (1 Corinthians 11:26).

There are things which happen in our lives that we would like to forget. But there are other events that we remember again and again with great pleasure.

Every now and again my wife Valerie and I take out our photographs and remember the wonderful holidays we have had. At other times we are saddened when we look at photographs of people who have died — people we miss.

At various times during the year the family gets together and much of the talk is about the good times the children had when they were growing up. Of course, someone usually says, 'Dad, do you remember when you smacked me and I didn't deserve it?' And sometimes I remind them of things they did — good and bad!

During the year we remember birthdays and usually presents are given and received. So it is important and pleasant to remember some special occasions.

On the farm where I grewup there was one job I didn't like very much — milking the cows. I found it a boring job and was always hoping the time would pass quickly so I could get out and do something else. I didn't want to become a farmer and early in life decided to become a schoolteacher. There are no cows to milk while teaching children!

Over the years I had forgotten just how much I disliked milking cows. But one day milking cows came flooding back to my mind. It is strange how something happens which brings back memories. I was in the laundry when Val put some bleach into a bucket of water. That bleach had the same smell as the bleach we put in the water we used to wash the cows' udders. In my mind I imagined sitting down washing the cows' teats before milking. I didn't like that memory at all. So I said to Val, 'I don't like the smell of that bleach. It reminds me of milking cows. The next time you buy bleach would you get some with a different smell, please?' Now we have lemon-scented bleach and I think it is much more pleasant!

The Scripture passage for today tells us that Christians should remember the death of the Lord Jesus Christ. The Bible teaches us that there is one way appointed by God in which we are to remember the saving death of Christ, and that is at the communion service.

The wine used in the communion service reminds us of the shed blood of Christ our Saviour. In those last few hours before his death, Jesus was very cruelly treated. When the soldiers whipped him the blood flowed from the wounds on his back. The crown of thorns cut his forehead and blood ran down his face. Then on the cross the nails punctured his hands and feet and blood dripped down to the ground from his wounds. Finally, a soldier thrust a spear into Christ's side and yet more blood flowed from his body. He suffered all of this so that his people might find forgiveness of sins.

Think about the words of Scripture: 'And according to the law almost all things are purged with blood, and without shedding of blood there is no remission' (Hebrews 9:22). Through the shed blood of our Saviour the sins of his people are forgiven. The fact that his blood was shed tells us that Christ's death was a violent one. The bread reminds us of the body of Christ, which was broken for his people. Christ's body was bruised and scarred as he bore the penalty for our sins.

The communion service is a wonderful meal of remembrance — a time to remember what the Lord Jesus Christ has done for us. Sitting at the Lord's Table is for Christians only, because they alone have experienced the forgiveness of sins and salvation.

The Lord's Supper should also remind us of another great truth — that one day our Saviour will come again and take us to be with himself. Truly the Lord's Supper is a wonderful way, appointed by God, to remember the love of Jesus Christ.

Activities

1. Why do Christians celebrate the Lord's Supper?
2. Who should sit at the Lord's Table?
3. Until what great event will Christians eat the Lord's Supper?

Death is not far away

.... Read ....
1 Samuel 20:1-11

'There is but a step between me and death' (1 Samuel 20:3).

David, who became King of Israel after King Saul's death, knew the truth of the words in our text. In fact it was he who spoke them. Saul wanted David dead and he did all he could to kill the one appointed by God to be king over Israel.

In today's Scripture passage we read of the love which existed between David and Saul's son Jonathan. It was Jonathan who warned David on this occasion that his father wanted him dead. If you read the whole chapter you will find out how David was able to escape from Saul's clutches. But David knew that death was his companion everywhere he travelled. We all need to understand that death is also our shadow, following us wherever we go. Unless the Lord Jesus returns beforehand, each one of us will die. None of us can avoid the day of our death. Truly, for all of us there is just a step between life and death. We are only a heartbeat away from facing Christ the Judge.

For most people death comes naturally when the years have rolled by. But no one can be sure when the moment of death will come.

Some time ago when I was travelling by bus to my brother's home I saw a car which had smashed into some street-lights. A hundred metres before we came to the lights we saw a wheel lying on the road. Then everyone on the bus saw police cars and two ambulances parked beside the smashed car. The car's roof had been torn off, the front had been smashed in and its rear end lay twenty metres or so from the front which was jammed hard against the metal lamppost.

I turned to the man sitting beside me and said, 'Well, I guess the people in that car are dead. No one could survive such a smash.' He agreed with me.

That night on the TV there was a report about the accident we had seen. Four young people had been in the car and to my amazement I heard that, while one man had been killed instantly, his three friends had escaped without any serious injury.

The young people had been out for the day, and I imagine the thought of death never entered their heads at all. Then in a moment one of them was dead — a young man had died instantly. He would never reach old age. He would never have another opportunity to repent of his sins and place his faith in Christ for his salvation. His life was over! There would be no second chance for that young man.

I have known several young people who died without even reaching their teens. No one can be sure of the day of his or her death.

Oh, reader, have you made preparations for the time of your death? The only preparation you can make is to truly repent of your sins and place your trust in Christ for your salvation. This very day — yes, right now — prepare for death. You may never get a second chance. Today may be the day of your death.

Activities

• •

1. How close is death to you?
2. What is death?
3. Name two people who have entered heaven without passing through death (see Genesis 5:24; 2 Kings 2:11-12).

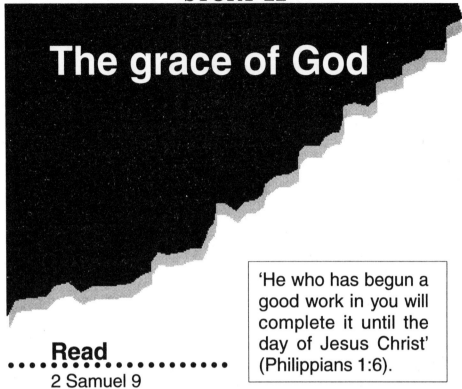

The grace of God

'He who has begun a
good work in you will
complete it until the
day of Jesus Christ'
(Philippians 1:6).

.... **Read** ....
2 Samuel 9

Our text reminds us that once God has begun the work of salvation in a person's heart, he will continue that work until one day the saved sinner enters heaven. The apostle Paul teaches this truth very clearly in Romans 8:29-30: 'For whom he foreknew, he also predestined to be conformed to the image of his Son... Moreover whom he predestined, these he also called; whom he called, these he also justified; and whom he justified, these he also glorified.'

Our God is gracious. Every person upon the face of the earth deserves hell because of sin. But God is a God of love. Instead of casting us all into hell, he decided to save a people. His grace is the undeserved mercy and love shown to sinners who deserved punishment.

And why should God save his people? After all, the penalty for sin had to be paid. It was Jesus who paid our debt. He came into the world to demonstrate God's love. He came to carry the sins of his people to the cross. He came and died in the place of his sinful people. One day all of God's people will be given glorious bodies, like the one Jesus had after his resurrection, in which they will enjoy the new creation and God's presence for ever.

God's grace is wonderful. For the sake of Jesus Christ our Saviour, God forgives our sins. But why should God take the trouble to bless us during our lives? And he does bless us greatly! Not only do we receive the necessities of life, but great spiritual blessings are ours as well. We have a true joy as we serve God. We rejoice in the knowledge that our sins are forgiven. God gives us a peace in our hearts because we realize that we are at peace with him. No longer is he angry with us. The Holy Spirit begins and continues with the work of making us Christlike. We are also fed spiritually when we read God's Word.

Once again we must ask the question: why should God be pleased to bless us when we deserve his anger? The answer is that God blesses us because of the saving work of his beloved Son who is our Saviour.

I trust you have read the Scripture passage for today, because it tells a wonderful story that illustrates the grace of God. King Saul was dead and David had become King of Israel. David's dear friend Jonathan, mentioned in the last story, was also dead. David wept over the loss of his friend and asked the question: 'Is there still anyone who is left of the house of Saul, that I may show him kindness for Jonathan's sake?' (v.1).

David had made a promise to Jonathan many years before, and now he would keep that promise. Turn again to the Bible reading from the last chapter and read the vow David made (1 Samuel 20:12-17).

David found a son of his friend Jonathan, named Mephibosheth who was lame in both feet. Then, for the sake of his dead friend, David took Mephibosheth to his home and from that day forward Mephibosheth always ate at the king's table.

David loved Jonathan and for the sake of his dear friend he looked after his son. What an act of love and kindness! What an act of grace! Mephibosheth didn't deserve a place at King David's table. However, for the sake of another, David showed him love.

Reader, this is the situation with God and his people. For the sake of Christ, God's beloved Son, we receive blessings we do not deserve. We cannot earn the blessings of God. God freely gives us blessings because of the work of the Son he loves. This is grace!

Have you experienced the grace of God in your life? May you be one of those who are loved by God for the sake of his Son Jesus Christ.

Activities

1. Find out all you can about Mephibosheth.
2. Why was King David kind to him?
3. Why does God show kindness to all who are Christians?
4. What is meant by 'the grace of God'?

I don't like the medicine

.... **Read** ....
Romans 3: 9-31

'For by grace you have been saved through faith, and that not of yourselves; it is the gift of God, not of works, lest anyone should boast' (Ephesians 2:8-9).

I'm sure my readers are just like me when it comes to most medicines and medical treatment — we don't like it very much!

I have had surgery quite a few times over the past ten years and never looked forward to the needles and medicines. Often the doctors prescribe medicine which tastes terrible. Once when I complained to a nurse she

said, 'If you don't drink it, I'll force it down your throat!' I very quietly drank my medicine. I'm sure that the more terrible the medicine tastes the better it works!

Another time a nurse was trying to get some blood out of my arm. She was having a lot of trouble finding the vein. After several tries my arm was feeling quite sore. I then jokingly suggested that as I had a big jugular vein in my neck she might find that easy to get blood from. She looked at me and said that if I didn't keep still and quiet she would do just that. So I kept very still and quiet as I wasn't sure whether she was joking or not.

For young people, there are a lot of medicines available today that taste quite good — they are flavoured with orange or peppermint, or something just as nice. When I have to give some medicine to my grandchildren they usually open their mouths wide and swallow without much trouble.

But when my brother and I were young there wasn't any sweet-tasting medicine. Many chemists made up their own mixtures and they weren't worried about the taste. It was left up to mums and dads to make sure their children took the medicine. I can still remember standing beside John, both of us with our mouths tightly closed and Mum saying, 'If you don't open wide and get this down, I'll call your father.' I can even remember once being held down while the medicine was poured into my mouth. Things were tough in those days!

But Mum had a sensible way of getting us to take medicine that didn't taste nice. She would cut an orange into pieces. Then with the spoonful of medicine at the ready she would say, 'Open wide and drink this down. Then suck the piece of orange. That will get rid of the awful taste.' So with an orange in one hand we would open our mouths and down the medicine would go. Then we would quickly suck the orange and its sweet taste would get rid of the nasty taste of the medicine.

When my children were growing up we used the same method to get them to take their medicine. 'Down the hatch and then pop a lolly into your mouth,' Val and I would say. This system usually worked. But whether the medicine tastes sweet or bitter, we all need it at some time to help cure our illnesses.

We have all been born with a deadly disease called sin. The consequence of this terrible condition is death, unless the Lord Jesus returns beforehand. But, praise God, there is a medicine available to deal with the sin disease. The cure for the deadly disease of sin is repentance and saving faith in the Lord Jesus Christ. This is the perfect remedy, but most people hate it. They don't want to repent of their sins and trust in the saving work of another. They want to avoid taking God's medicine for sin.

Men and women are proud and want to do something to earn their salvation. They don't want to depend on the work of Jesus Christ. So they set out to do good works, trying to earn their way to heaven. This might make them feel good, but good works will not save anyone. Today's Bible reading teaches us this truth very clearly.

Sometimes ministers try to change the medicine for sin to make it taste better. They tell people lies. 'Why,' they say, 'God is a God of love. He won't hurt anyone. Everyone will get to heaven. Just be happy and enjoy yourself.'

But there is only one way to deal with sin and that is to go humbly to the Lord Jesus Christ, confessing your sins and trusting in him and his saving work alone. It means looking away from anything you might have done and not trusting in your own works. It means giving up sinful practices and living according to the law of God. In this way you show Christ that you love him.

We are told in our text that the only way of salvation — faith in Christ — is the gift of God. Salvation is there for the taking, without cost to the sinner. Jesus has paid the cost.

Have you taken the medicine for sin? There is only one medicine and it cannot be sweetened. It has always been the old, old story, of the love of God as found in Jesus Christ. May God bless you all.

Activities

• •

1. Discuss today's text to make sure you all understand what is being taught.
2. What is meant by 'faith in Christ'?
3. What is wrong with the statement: 'God is a God of love. Everyone will reach heaven'?

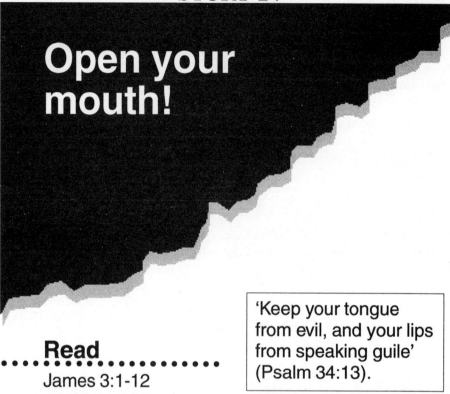

Open your mouth!

.... Read ....
James 3:1-12

'Keep your tongue from evil, and your lips from speaking guile' (Psalm 34:13).

I'm sure we all appreciate our mouths. We need them for eating and drinking and for talking. Some people have to breathe through their mouths. Lips can be used to hold things or teeth to break a piece of sticky tape, for example. Indeed the mouth has many great uses (though we need to be very careful as some children have had nasty accidents through putting things in their mouths and then swallowing them by mistake).

If you have read the text for today as well as the Scripture passage you will realize that the mouth can be used for evil purposes. I know some children who bite others. I have seen people spitting, which isn't very nice. Sometimes I have seen rude people poking their tongues out at other people. And, worst of all, people sometimes tell lies or say unkind things about other people.

Now, you all know that you must keep your teeth in good repair, or you will end up with false teeth. So you clean your teeth and visit the dentist regularly to have your teeth checked. If any holes are found then fillings must go in. I don't think many people enjoy visiting the dentist for repair work.

Our children were taken to the dentist on a regular basis. Occasionally there was work to be done, but most of the time they had a good report about the state of their teeth. I would like to tell you a story about one of our girls who was to visit the dentist for her annual check-up.

Heather was about five years of age and she was due for a visit to the dentist's. When she climbed into the chair the dentist asked her to open her mouth. But Heather seemed frightened and through her clenched teeth she replied, 'No.'

'Come on,' the dentist continued. 'I just want to have a look at your teeth. This won't hurt at all.'

But Heather just kept her mouth closed, and through her tightly clenched teeth repeated, 'No.'

The dentist told my wife to make another appointment. He suggested that when Heather arrived for the new appointment he would give her a tablet to calm her nerves. He was sure there would be no problem then.

The day arrived for the second visit to the dentist. Heather seemed happy and unconcerned about seeing him. She knew that this time she had to open her mouth. The dentist's nurse gave her a tablet and soon Heather was in the chair, with her mouth wide open, and the dentist was looking at her teeth.

'Yes,' he said, 'there is a small hole. I'll fill it now and get it over and done with.'

Looking at Heather, the dentist then said, 'I'll give you an injection to stop any pain. The needle won't hurt. It will just be a tiny prick.' The injection was given and soon the dentist was ready to begin drilling.

'Open your mouth now, Heather,' the dentist said gently.

But Heather just clenched her teeth very tightly and said, 'No!' No matter how we tried, we couldn't get her to open her mouth. The dentist told us we would have to make another appointment, but also said that as he had given her an injection we would have to pay for it. We paid the bill and made another appointment.

When we arrived home, I took Heather aside, slapped her bottom and told her that the next time she had better open her mouth, or she would miss out on some of the good things the rest of the family would have. On the third visit to the dentist everything went well. The mouth was opened wide, the tooth was filled and never again did Heather refuse to open her mouth for the dentist.

Reader, there is a time to open your mouth and a time to close it. If you are going to say something kind, then open your mouth and say it. If you want to praise God, then open your mouth and praise him. But if you are about to say something hurtful, then keep your mouth shut.

The apostle Paul wrote these important words: 'Let no corrupt communication proceed out of your mouth, but what is good for necessary edification, that it may impart grace to the hearers' (Ephesians 4:29).

On Judgement Day each of us will have to give an account to Christ the Judge concerning the words we have spoken. Jesus' words should make us very careful about how we speak for he said, 'But I say to you that for every idle word men may speak, they will give account of it in the day of judgement. For by your words you will be justified, and by your words you will be condemned' (Matthew 12:36-37). How we need to place a guard upon our mouths!

Activities

● ●

1. How will you feel when Jesus asks you to explain all that you have said during your life?
2. What sort of speech should come from your mouth?
3. 'If you can't say something nice about a person, then say nothing.' What does this mean?

I'm not going to drown yet!

Read
1 Corinthians 9:24-27

'Therefore we also, since we are surrounded by so great a cloud of witnesses, let us lay aside every weight, and the sin which so easily ensnares us, and let us run with endurance the race that is set before us, looking unto Jesus, the author and finisher of our faith...' (Hebrews 12:1-2).

In my earlier books I have written about some of my adventures out on the ocean, trying to catch the really big fish. Fishing out at sea can be a dangerous sport. Not only is there a real danger from sharks that sometimes take an unhealthy interest in small boats, but sometimes huge whales come very close too. When this happens the outboard motor is started and I move away to safer waters.

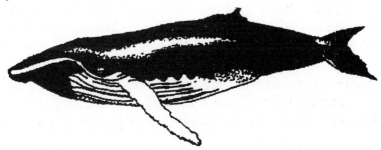

An event happened at sea that always reminds my brother and me about the words found in today's text. The apostle Paul here looks at the Christian life as a great race. I imagine he was thinking about the Olympic Games, or other local sports events which were held in his part of the world. Athletes who take part in the modern Olympics compete for the glory of winning and the hope of receiving a gold, silver or bronze medal. Of course, there is a real thrill to all who take part in the Olympic Games, but each competitor really trains to win. The old saying is so true: 'Winners are grinners.'

Looking at pictures of the early Olympic Games you will notice that the athletes dressed very differently from those of today. Modern athletes wear skin-tight clothing that will not catch the air and slow the person down. Some swimmers even shave their heads in the hope that they can gain just a fraction of a second's advantage over their competitors. In the ancient Olympics athletes ran naked. Nothing would hinder them as they competed for the prize — a laurel wreath.

One day my brother John and I were out at sea catching some very big fish. During the day, we noticed that the ocean swells were getting bigger and bigger. We were later to find out that a couple of days before, some 400 kilometres away, a mini-cyclone had created huge waves. The swells had taken several days to reach our part of the world. At midday John suggested that it might be best if we set out for home.

About a kilometre from the mouth of the river we saw huge waves breaking over the bar. (As I explained in one of my earlier books, the wind and tides cause sand to build up at the mouth of the river and the area of shallow water over this sand is known as 'the bar'.) Crossing the bar on the way out had been no problem as then there had been hardly any ocean swell.

To our horror, the closer we came to the river-mouth, the bigger the waves looked. John and I didn't know what to do. We thought that it would be a great risk to try to cross the bar with the waves so huge. But we had to get back into the river because our car and trailer were parked not far from the river-mouth. After half an hour of driving the boat back and forwards outside the breaking waves we decided that we would have to try to get in, even if we capsized in the attempt.

John then asked for a life-jacket. First of all, he started to take off his clothes. I just watched him as he stripped down to his underpants. 'What are you doing?' I asked him with a strange look on my face.

'If I get tossed into the water, I'm not going to have anything on me that will drag me to the bottom of the ocean,' he replied.

Soon I was in the same state of undress and together we headed for the mouth of the river. As it happened, we need not have worried. We put the boat behind a big wave and simply followed it over the bar. When it broke we raced the boat through the froth and into the safety of the calm river.

The apostle Paul saw the Christian life as a race. The finishing-line for the Christian is heaven in the presence of Christ. The Christian runs to win a prize which is eternal life with Christ. And Christians must run well.

The Christian life involves faithfulness to God. It means that we must turn away from sin and obey the God who loves us. Sin must be rooted out of our lives because sin is the work of Satan. We are to live in such a way that Christ is glorified. Sin does not have the victory if we belong to Christ, because by his Spirit God has broken its power. So we run the Christian life looking unto Jesus, and not at the things of the world that would cause us to stumble and fall.

Are you running the Christian race seriously? If not there will be no prize at the end of your life. Follow Jesus in all his ways and get rid of the sin that is found in your life. Trust yourself to Christ as the only one who can save you. The crown of life will then be yours and you will eternally enjoy God's new creation. Then you will enjoy the love of God and be able to serve God perfectly. May God give everyone who reads these words a saving faith in his Son Jesus Christ.

Activities

● ●

1. What race is the Christian running?
2. How are Christians to run that race?
3. What is the prize at the end of the race?

A badly damaged image

....**Read**............
Genesis 1:26-31

'Then God said, "Let us make man in our image, according to our likeness..." So God created man in his own image; in the image of God he created him; male and female he created them' (Genesis 1:26-27).

My class once presented me with a moulded image of myself. For a long time I had it sitting on my study table, as I appreciated that particular class of boys, and especially their sense of humour. I don't know what happened to that bust, but somehow over the years it has been lost.

I'm useless when it comes to moulding things. I don't have the ability to make recognizable shapes out of clay, but I have encouraged many children to have a go. In fact some of my pupils did quite well.

With some help, several of the boys sculptured what they thought was a figure that looked like me. They were very proud of their work and decided to paint the bust and have it fired and glazed. The intention of the class was to present me with the finished work at the end-of-year assembly. But the person responsible for the firing dropped the figure. The side of the head was flattened and the face was pushed out of shape.

Instead of being upset about the damage, the boys decided that the ruined figure should still be fired and glazed. At the annual school assembly I was presented with a well-painted and glazed, but very much damaged, bust of myself. Everyone had a good laugh, but somehow that figure was very important to me. For many years that damaged figure reminded me of a very likeable class of boys. Even though it was damaged everyone could recognize that it was meant to represent a face and some people claimed that they could see a resemblance to me.

Today's text tells us very plainly that God created Adam in his own image. Adam was holy and loved God. And like God, man was made to rule. Adam was to be God's appointed ruler of the earth.

God moulded Adam from the dust of the earth. When God breathed life into Adam he declared that his creation was very good. The boys who moulded that bust no doubt thought the same about their work. But just as the sculpture was damaged when it fell, so also Adam was greatly hurt when he and Eve fell into sin. Adam's sin brought death upon all his descendants.

Even though God's image in Adam was greatly spoilt by sin, there remained a resemblance to God, Adam's Creator. Like the damaged bust presented to me by my class, Adam still retained something of his original likeness. Just as I could never repair the damage that the fall caused to the sculpture, neither could any human repair the damage done by sin to the human race.

Jesus Christ is the last Adam (1 Corinthians 15:45). He came into this world to do what the first Adam should have done. He lived a life of total obedience to his Father. Through faith in the last Adam, the Lord Jesus Christ, sinners can find eternal life. Paul wrote, 'For as in Adam all die, even so in Christ all shall be made alive' (1 Corinthians 15:22).

Today humans still bear the image of the first Adam. We are sinners, but the Holy Spirit has broken sin's grip and Christians are being moulded into the likeness of their Saviour, Jesus Christ. Paul tells us another wonderful truth: 'And as we have borne the image of the man of dust, we shall also bear the image of the heavenly Man' (1 Corinthians 15:49).

I often say, 'I'm not perfect yet, but one day I will be.' And this is true for all of God's people. One day the work of remoulding into the likeness of Christ will be complete. When we pass into the presence of our Lord and Saviour we shall be made perfectly holy (Hebrews 12:23). This must be the case, for we are told that 'without holiness no one will see the Lord' (Hebrews 12:14). And the holiness we shall have will be the perfection of Christ given to us for clothing (Hebrews 12:10). Speaking of Christ the King who would save his people, the prophet Jeremiah said he would be called 'the LORD our Righteousness' (Jeremiah 23:6).

It is my prayer that each one who reads these words may be united by faith to the one who can save sinners.

Activities

■■■

1. In whose image was man created? How did Adam resemble God?
2. What damaged God's image in man?
3. Who is the perfect man?
4. When shall we be truly like Christ?

A man in heaven

....Read............
Revelation 5

'Now when he had spoken these things, while they watched, he was taken up, and a cloud received him out of their sight' (Acts 1:9).

How many times have you gone somewhere and returned with something you didn't have before you left? I'm sure you are like me and this has happened many times to you.

One of the most rewarding events in my life was the day I graduated from university. I carried out my studies while I was teaching and this meant a lot of work. We had a young family at the time and Val had to sacrifice much in order that I could have the time necessary for my studies. We didn't get out very often and I always had a lot of studying to do. At one time it was necessary for me to be away from home for a month to do some research. While I was spending days at a large city library pouring over old books and newspapers Val was caring for the children at home. But we both knew that all the effort would one day prove its worth.

Then the day came when I was to graduate from the university. I can still remember the university chancellor

saying that many of the degrees being presented to students should have been presented to both husbands and wives. In my case I knew this was very true.

Up till that point of time I had attended classes at the university during the evening dressed in my ordinary clothes, but on the day of my graduation all was different. I was dressed up in my academic gown, with a very colourful hood around my shoulders. I also wore a mortar board with a tassel hanging to one side. I think I looked very smart as my photograph was taken! Then some of the family dressed up in my academic clothes and had their photographs taken as well. But now I really had something I didn't have before. I had my university degree and the right to wear my academic gown.

I tell this story to introduce a wonderful truth concerning the Lord Jesus Christ. I want us to think about what happened when Christ left heaven and took a body when he was born of the virgin Mary. This meant that on earth Christ had something he didn't have before leaving heaven. He had a body that was put to death.

But he rose from the tomb, destroying the power of death. And after the resurrection he was seen by many people. He still had a body — one that could be touched, that could eat food and yet that could pass through the walls of a room without using the door (John 20:19).

Do you remember Thomas, who was not present when Christ first appeared to his disciples a week after the resurrection? He could not believe what he was told about Christ. He said he would not only have to see the resurrected Lord, but would have to touch his body before he could believe that Christ was alive. When he appeared a week later Jesus said to Thomas, 'Reach your finger here, and look at my hands; and reach your hand here, and put it into my side. Do not be unbelieving, but believing' (John 20:27). Thomas then believed and answered, 'My Lord and my God!' (John 20:28).

Luke records that the disciples were terrified when they were met by Jesus. They thought he was a spirit. But Jesus said, 'Behold my hands and my feet, that it is I myself. Handle me and see, for a spirit does not have flesh and bones as you see I have' (Luke 24:39).

This is the Jesus who ascended to heaven and is described in our reading for today as the 'Lamb' of God and also as 'the Lion of the tribe of Judah' (Revelation 5:5-6). He is now in heaven and he took back to heaven something that he did not have when he left to come to earth: he took a human body because he is both God and man in the one person. So when you pray remember that the Lord Jesus Christ is in heaven, sitting upon the throne of God. He has a body. There is a man in heaven!

There in heaven Christ takes our prayers and presents them to his Father. That same Jesus Christ also pours out blessings upon all people — especially those who belong to him.

And as surely as Christ is in heaven in a glorious resurrected body, so also all of his people will one day be there too. We shall have glorified bodies similar to that of the Lord Jesus Christ.

Think about it, Christian brothers and sisters. There is today a man in heaven and that God-man is your Saviour and mine. Praise the Lord!

Activities

● ●

1. What thoughts do you think went through the minds of the disciples and the women when they found the empty tomb?
2. What does the resurrection of Jesus Christ mean to you?
3. Philippians 2:5-11 is a wonderful passage of Scripture. What does it teach?
4. What do you think the resurrection body of the saints will be like?

I won't gey thrown off!

Read
Read Matthew
6:30-35,69-75

> *'And I give them eternal life, and they shall never perish; neither shall anyone snatch them out of my hand'* (John 10:28).

The apostle Peter was a great saint, but despite his confidence that he would be faithful to Christ in all circumstances, we find that he denied his Saviour. However, Christ didn't refuse to have anything more to do with Peter, but brought him to repentance and then sent him out to preach the gospel to unsaved people. In the Bible we read of other occasions when Peter fell into sin, but each time he repented and continued to serve Christ faithfully.

Children who live in cities must often wish they could live on a farm. Farm life is so different from city life and can be most enjoyable. Horse-

riding is one aspect of country life that can be great fun!

When I was young we had horses and almost every day John and I would spend time riding about the farm. Most of our horses were quiet animals who could be trusted with anyone. They would trot about and there was never any fear of falling off. Rarely did they ever buck. So John and I felt sure that we were good in the saddle. On those rare occasions when a horse reared up we would stick in the saddle. Our confidence in our horse-riding was really great — until Dad bought a new horse.

The horse's name was Dick. At first he seemed quite friendly, but before long he started to show a nasty streak in his character. When we approached him to put on his bridle he would put his head down and make a run at us. We would have to dive through the fence to avoid being trampled.

One day John and I caught Dick and, full of confidence in our riding ability — our stickability in the saddle — we set out to round up the cows for Dad. But Dick had other ideas! He allowed us to catch him and put on the saddle and bridle. However, when we both climbed on his back and turned him in the direction of the cattle, he swung round and bolted for the other side of the paddock.

Now, as I have already said, John and I were both quite good riders and we felt sure that we would be safe, even though the wind was whistling through our hair a little faster than usual.

Then, without warning, Dick stopped dead and over his head we went! We both returned home with tears in our eyes and patches of skin missing. Our horse-riding confidence was shattered. Never again did we trust Dick. He tried the same stunt again and again. After a few more falls we went back to riding our quiet ponies — it was a lot safer.

Despite all our confidence and our horse-riding ability there were times when Dick threw us to the ground. The Christian life can be like that. We may have all the confidence in the world. We may also know the Scriptures and love the Lord. But the devil is there, tempting us to sin. And, sadly, we fall into sin as Peter did.

But Christ does not leave us there. He has made that precious promise that if we are his people — if we have been given eternal life — then no one

can pluck us out of his hand. My horse-riding depended upon my own ability. My safety in Christ depends entirely upon him. He has complete authority in heaven and on earth (Matthew 28:18) and can bring to pass everything he has promised.

Jesus went on to stress that it was not only his power that kept the saints safe, but the almighty power of God, his Father. He said, speaking of the safety of his people, 'My Father, who has given them to me, is greater than all; and no one is able to snatch them out of my Father's hand. I and my Father are one' (John 10:29-30).

The apostle Paul, describing the Christian's security in Christ, said, 'For I am persuaded that neither death nor life, nor angels nor principalities nor powers, nor things present nor things to come, nor height nor depth, nor any other created thing, shall be able to separate us from the love of God which is in Christ Jesus our Lord' (Romans 8:38-39).

This is real security. Our safety depends upon God, not upon our feeble strength. God has hold of his people and he will never let us go.

Peter is a wonderful example of Christ's faithfulness. After denying that he was a follower of Christ Peter wept many tears of sorrow and repentance. But Jesus was not going to cast Peter aside. Peter was one of his believing people. Christ had a job for Peter to carry out. After the resurrection Christ faced Peter and three times asked him the question: 'Simon, son of Jonah, do you love me?' (John 21:15-19). Three times Peter answered, 'Yes,' to that question. The question was asked three times because Peter had denied Christ three times.

Peter truly repented of his sin and went on to give much faithful service to his Saviour. Christ held on to Peter, as he does to all his people. None who have been given to him by the Father will be lost. And all who trust in Jesus for salvation have tasted the goodness of the Saviour who said, 'Come to me, all you who labour and are heavy laden, and I will give you rest. Take my yoke upon you and learn from me, for I am gentle and lowly in heart, and you will find rest for your souls. For my yoke is easy and my burden is light' (Matthew 11:28-30).

My ability to stick on a horse depended upon me and let me down. Jesus Christ will never let me down! And he will never let down any who have placed their faith in him.

Activities

● ●

1. Find out all you can about the apostle Peter.
2. How do you think Peter died? (Read John 21:18).
3. Why is Christ all-powerful?
4. Why can God's people be sure they will never be lost?

I'm a millionaire!

Read

Malachi 3:8-12

'He who has pity on the poor lends to the LORD, and he will pay back what he has given' (Proverbs 19:17).

The Bible teaches us that God does not owe us anything. Whenever we do something for the Lord he is never in our debt. After all, if we could live a life of serving God perfectly, we would simply have done what we should have done. But our God is very gracious and he repays his people for all their faithfulness and works done in his name. God doesn't owe us anything at all, but out of his pure grace he rewards his people for all they do.

Our Bible reading is the challenge that God gave his people before the birth of Christ. The Jews had turned away from serving the Lord and they were experiencing the punishment of God. Through the prophet Malachi, God reminded them that they had not given him their tithes. They had in fact stolen from God.

They probably thought to themselves, 'Times are hard and we need everything we have just to survive. How can we afford to give anything to the work of the Lord?'

Others may have said to themselves, 'God doesn't really care about the situation we are in. If he did we would have rain and the crops would grow. Why bother giving a tithe to the Lord's works? God isn't interested in us.'

But God was interested. He challenged the people to put him to the test. The challenge simply was: 'Give your tithe to the temple so that my worship may be carried out properly and then I will bless you beyond anything you can imagine.' What a challenge! God is no man's debtor. Had the Jewish people accepted God's challenge they would have been greatly blessed.

Today Christians serve the Lord in many ways and God never overlooks what they do in Christ's name. I'm sure that on Judgement Day when God rewards his people there will be many who receive praise from him for doing good works of which they were not even conscious.

Some time ago I read a lovely story in the newspaper of a young woman who always spoke to an old lady sitting on the verandah of the house in which she lived. Sometimes she would stop and talk for a long time. She knew the old lady was lonely so she made a habit of leaving home a little earlier each morning so they could talk for a few minutes. Sometimes she even took the old lady a bunch of flowers. They became friends, but the young woman didn't even know the old lady's name.

The newspaper article told how the old lady died and the friendly young woman found out that she had been left all the lady's possessions. The old lady was a millionaire, who had no relatives. The newspaper reported that the young woman was overjoyed at what had happened. She said she had no idea that the lady was wealthy and all she had done was to speak each day to an old lady in an effort to give her some happiness. That old lady did not owe the kind young woman anything, but she rewarded her for her kind actions beyond anything she could have imagined.

And this is how our God works. Do you remember the words of Jesus, found in Matthew 25:40? Jesus had been telling his disciples great truths, and one of them was that anything done in his name to a fellow believer was just the same as having done it to himself. He said, 'Inasmuch as you did it to one of the least of these my brethren, you did it to me.' To these people Christ will say on Judgement Day: 'Come you blessed of my Father, inherit the kingdom prepared for you from the foundation of the world' (Matthew 25:34).

And what a wonderful kingdom that will be! All Christ's people will see him face to face. What a joy that will be! And of this kingdom we read, 'And God will wipe away every tear from their eyes; there shall be no more death, nor sorrow, nor crying; and there shall be no more pain, for the former things have passed away' (Revelation 21:4). Heaven is the land of perfection because it is the land of perfect holiness. Since there is no more sin there can be no more sorrow, sickness or death.

Reader, do you have a home in this glorious kingdom which God has prepared for his people?

Activities

• •

1. What is meant by the 'tithe'?
2. Why do church members give money to the church?
3. List five wonderful things about heaven.
4. Who will be in heaven?

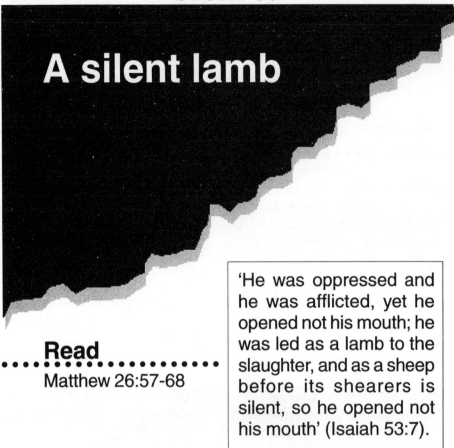

A silent lamb

Read

Matthew 26:57-68

'He was oppressed and he was afflicted, yet he opened not his mouth; he was led as a lamb to the slaughter, and as a sheep before its shearers is silent, so he opened not his mouth' (Isaiah 53:7).

When I went to primary school I can only remember going on one excursion, and that was to the zoo. Outings were not very popular in schools when I was young. But today everything is different. It seems as if my grandchildren spend more time away from school than in the classroom. They attend camps, and many excursions to places of interest are always being talked about. One grandson, Michael, spends a lot of time away from school as he has done really well at hockey. He has played in the state team, attended many training camps and played in many games. Life at school seems much more exciting today than when I was young, and children today seem to have a wider knowledge of things than in my schooldays.

As a teacher, I was involved in taking children on excursions, as well as school camps. One excursion I will never forget was when I took my class to the zoo. Several parents volunteered to come along. Everyone had a long and tiring day. But was it exciting? The children saw animals they had only read about.

But the greatest thrill of the day was when we reached the gorilla cage. The gorilla was standing at the front of the cage hanging onto the bars. The class lined up several metres from the cage and talked to the gorilla. They all seemed to know gorilla language! With the children, standing in the front row, was one of the parents — a minister's wife. I know she hasn't forgotten that excursion!

Suddenly the gorilla bent down, scooped up a handful of muck from the bottom of his cage and threw it at her. The poor lady was covered from head to toe in a stinking mess. The children couldn't help laughing.

Then the gorilla picked up another handful of muck and threw it at them. That put an end to their laughing! As the gorilla then turned and walked away I thought I could see a smile on his face!

Another time I took the class to the local abattoirs. We were able to see the whole process, from the slaughter of the animals to the packing of the meat into boxes ready for transport to the butchers and shops. Some of the children didn't like what they saw and felt ill. Some even went outside and sat under a tree. They were distressed at seeing animals killed.

Some children spent a little time patting some of the sheep. I guess they felt sorry for the little animals about to be killed. The sheep and other animals didn't know what was going to happen to them. They made no sound as they were driven into the yard to be slaughtered. The killing was instantaneous.

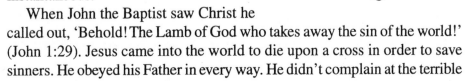

When John the Baptist saw Christ he called out, 'Behold! The Lamb of God who takes away the sin of the world!' (John 1:29). Jesus came into the world to die upon a cross in order to save sinners. He obeyed his Father in every way. He didn't complain at the terrible treatment handed out to him by the Roman soldiers and the leaders of the Jews. He was like a lamb about to be slaughtered. Had he wished, Jesus could have called upon the angels of heaven to come to his assistance, but he did not do so.

Silently he was led to the place of execution. He made no complaints. He asked his Father to forgive those who were harming him. He was concerned for Mary, his mother. From the cross he asked the apostle John to take care of her. He saved a repentant thief.

Jesus, the Lamb of God, fulfilled the prophecy of Isaiah 53 completely. The lambs sacrificed in the temple by the priests pointed to his sacrifice on the cross. But our Saviour, the Lamb of God, is also the King of kings, 'the Lion of the tribe of Judah' (Revelation 5:5).

One day the angels and the redeemed sinners will surround the throne of God and sing:

> Worthy is the Lamb who was slain
> To receive power and riches and wisdom,
> And strength and honour and glory and blessing! ...
> Blessing and honour and glory and power
> Be to him who sits on the throne,
> And to the Lamb, for ever and ever!
>
> (Revelation 5:12-13).

Oh, reader, will you be among that great number who sing this song of praise to God and Jesus Christ, the Lamb of God?

Activities

● ●

1. What name is given to the workplace where animals are killed and prepared for humans to eat?
2. Name some animals to which Jesus is likened. Discuss these descriptions of Christ.
3. Why is Jesus called 'the King of kings'?

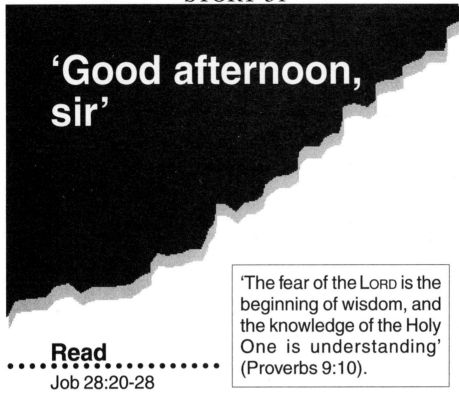

'Good afternoon, sir'

Read
Job 28:20-28

'The fear of the LORD is the beginning of wisdom, and the knowledge of the Holy One is understanding' (Proverbs 9:10).

We all like to think we are wise people. Of course, we make wrong decisions at times, but most of the time we like to think we make sensible ones. However, this is not always the case. Because we do not know everything, we can never be sure that the decisions we make are the best.

There is only one who is perfectly wise, and that is God. Paul said of our God that he alone is wise (Romans 16:27). God is the only one who has perfect knowledge of all things. Not only does he know everything, but he controls all events that take place. God is almighty beyond our imagination. He created the world by simply speaking the word. Now that is power! Our God is a God of grace, mercy and love. He is also a God who is perfectly holy and just in all his ways.

Today very few people fear God. But Jesus warned his hearers with these words: 'And do not fear those who kill the body but cannot kill the soul. But rather fear him who is able to destroy both soul and body in hell' (Matthew 10:28).

Before I became a Christian I feared God with a terrible fear. I knew I was a sinner and had broken God's law. I also knew that God would one day throw me into hell because of my sins. I was terrified of God's anger. If I could, I would have hidden myself from God so that he could never find me. Now this is fear, but not a good type of fear.

I remember a dog we once had who chased and killed a fowl. He was given a good smack for what he had done. For days after that whenever someone spoke loudly to him he put his tail between his legs and crouched down on the ground. He was terrified when he heard loud voices. I guess he thought he was in trouble and would get another smack. To fear God in that way is not the type of fear spoken of either in our text or in our reading from Job. It may be, however, that to be terrified of God is good because it could result in a true and proper fear of God.

What, then, is the fear of God spoken about in our text? I would like to tell you about it. What follows really happened to me and a small group of children who lived in the country and attended a school with just two teachers.

We were advised that the Governor General of Australia was to visit a city some miles from the school where I was teaching. All the children in the area were asked to gather in the showground and there the Governor General would drive through the rows of children. They would see close up the Australian representative of the Queen of England. This man was a 'Lord...' and he was held in awe by most people.

As many of the children in my school were young I decided that we wouldn't go to the city gathering because it would be too tiring for them. However, we would stand on the roadside and wave as the Governor General drove past our school.

We were standing on the grass beside the main road when we saw several police cars coming. Following them were four or five police on their motorcycles. Then there were several cars and more police cycles. I told the children to get ready to wave. As we were about to start waving, the police guard came to a stop on the road in front of our school. Then the police stepped out of their cars and stopped the traffic travelling in both directions on the road.

I had a very funny feeling in my stomach. The other schoolteacher, who was standing beside me, said, 'I think the Governor General's car is stopping.'

My wife Valerie said, 'Now don't forget to bow your head to him and call him "Sir".'

Sure enough, the Governor General's car stopped in front of the children. A man dressed in military uniform got out and came around to open the car door for the passenger to alight. I didn't expect anything like this to happen. I reminded the children to be very polite to this very important man.

The Governor General, dressed in his official clothes, stepped out of the car, walked across the grass and came over to me and the children. My heart trembled as I realized I was in the presence of the queen's representative. He didn't have to tell me who he was. I just nodded my head to him and said, 'Sir, this is a wonderful surprise. Thank you for stopping to speak to the children.'

I think my knees were trembling in his presence. I didn't have my tail between my legs like that frightened dog, but there was a fear in my heart. Many thoughts raced through my mind as I introduced each child to the Governor General. The children also had a type of fear in their hearts. They weren't frightened by the man, because he spoke so kindly to them. But they wondered why such a great man would stop to speak to them. The Governor General even went over and spoke to my wife.

He asked the children about the school and the farms where they lived. He then told them to be good students. After shaking my hand again he got back into his official car and everyone moved off. All the traffic which had been stopped by the police began to move again. My heart was filled with awe at what had happened.

This is the type of fear that our text speaks about. The wise person is one who has repented of his or her sins and loves God. When the repentant sinner begins to understand that the all-powerful God is his Father he knows a great sense of awe and wonder. The more you learn about your God, the more your heart will be filled with awe that God should love you and save you. A true knowledge of God will cause you to love him more and more.

Read your Bible. Speak to God in prayer. Let your heart be filled with amazement that God loves sinners. Now, are you one of the sinners loved by God? I pray that this is so.

Activities

1. What is the 'beginning of wisdom' and what does it mean?
2. Why should sinners be terrified of God?
3. How do you know that God loves sinners?

STORY 32

An almighty God

Read

Job 38:4-11

'To whom then will you liken God? Or what likeness will you compare to him?' (Isaiah 40:18).

When I was a teacher, there were times when I took my class out of school and we all lay down on the ground gazing up into the heavens. We would look at the clouds, the sun and the trees all around us and then talk about the wonder of God's creation. When we had school camps, we would do the same at night-time. We would talk about the stars hanging in endless

108

space. Our minds could not comprehend the majesty of the creation and the almighty power of God who created all things. I believe everyone should take a long, serious look at the world around us. Then we shall have some understanding of the glory of our God.

In Psalm 19:1 we read, 'The heavens declare the glory of God; and the firmament shows his handiwork.' When we begin to understand something about the God who created all things we shall say with the psalmist, 'O LORD, our Lord, how excellent is your name in all the earth!' (Psalm 8:1). When people look at the creation around them they have no excuse for saying that there is no God. All the evidence is there for a God of wisdom and almighty power.

I once had an experience that impressed upon my heart the greatness of God. I decided to spend a night by myself out at sea. I was sure that the really big fish would bite during the night. I felt uneasy on the ocean in the darkness. Every time there was a sound in the water I thought it might be a whale or a huge shark about to overturn the boat.

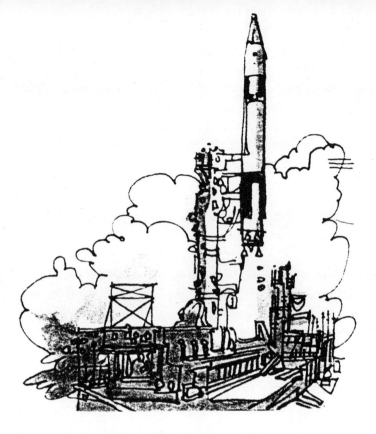

But there was something special about that particular night. It was 17 April 1970 and Apollo 13 was returning to earth after an explosion on board. There was a real danger that the astronauts might die in space. I had my radio with me and listened to the reports being broadcast about that exciting trip back to earth.

The sky was very clear as there were no clouds about. The heavens were exceptionally black and this caused the thousands of stars to shine brightly. I had my fishing-line over the side of the boat, which was just drifting about on the ocean. I felt tired so I lay down on the bottom and looked up into the heavens.

I tried to imagine what those astronauts were feeling as they hurtled through space. I looked at the stars for an hour or so thinking about the immensity of space. Space is endless. And hanging out there in space were stars and planets. I tried to image what it must have been like when God created the universe. My mind could not take in the power of my God who just spoke the word causing the worlds to burst into being — out of nothing. I thought of the power of my God who keeps the universe going. I just couldn't understand it all. But my heart was filled with awe and wonder at the might, glory and wisdom of the Creator God. I could tell all this by simply looking at the creation about me.

It was great to finally hear the news that the spacemen were safely back on earth. I knew that up in space they had seen something of the wonders of creation. But the greatest wonder concerning our God is that he has not just revealed himself in the creation around us, but has seen fit to reveal himself in the Scriptures. We can read about the power and majesty of God in the Bible.

But, even better than that, God has revealed himself to sinners in the person of his Son, Jesus Christ. In Christ we see the grace, mercy and love of the almighty God who created all things. The all-powerful God who created everything is not a God who just lives somewhere out there in space, but one who has come into the world to save sinners. God, who is perfectly holy, is interested in sinners like you and me. He invites sinners to come to him through Jesus Christ and be saved.

Oh, reader, have you any true understanding of the wonder, glory, power and grace of the Lord God? May he be pleased to reveal himself to you, not just as the God of creation, but also as the God of salvation.

Activities

• •

1. How do you know that there is a God?
2. God is wise. How do we know this?
3. How big is the universe?
4. Who keeps the universe going?

Take care of us when we are old, please!

Read
Psalm 71:9-18

'Now also when I am old and grey-headed, O God, do not forsake me...' (Psalm 71:18).

I'm sure that many of you who read these words find it hard to believe that one day you will be old. You may be young and able to run about without any trouble. You may be bursting with energy, but if you live long enough the day will come when your body begins to wear out. Then you won't be able to do all the things you do today.

It seems only yesterday that I was young, attending school, playing football and doing all the things young boys do. But the years have rolled by and now I sometimes find it a little difficult to get out of bed. Today's text speaks of the grey-headed people. I don't think I shall be grey-headed as my hair is falling out. One day I shall have grown completely through my hair and so have a nice shiny bald top. But I have no desire to be young again. I'm much closer to heaven than I was when I was young, and so is Valerie.

Some time ago I was talking to one of our daughters and said to her, 'Mum and I are starting to feel our age. We can't do the things we used to do. Should we begin to think about booking into a home for senior citizens?' Several times my wife and I had spoken about what the future might hold for both of us.

To our question our daughter replied, 'No. You live in your home as long as you can. We'll look after you when you can't look after yourself.'

112

This was comforting to hear, because old age can be a problem to the one getting old as well as the family responsible for looking after the ageing person.

A young granddaughter was listening to the conversation. Jessica had been showing us her new baby rabbit. She was very excited about getting a new white rabbit and we knew it was being lovingly looked after. She began telling us how she and her brother were looking after their baby rabbits. We asked her what they did with the rabbits at night-time.

'We put them out in their cage and throw a rug over it to keep them warm,' she replied.

'And what will you do for your nan and pop when we are old?' Valerie asked her.

'We'll throw a rug over you to keep you warm,' she replied.

Now old age brings a lot of problems for some people. Many old people become forgetful and this causes great concern. Some are simply unable to look after themselves and must be placed in a home or hospital where they can be cared for by nurses and others. And, sad to say, there are many old people who are very lonely because they have been forgotten by their families. They live alone in their homes and spend most of their time watching TV.

But God's people need never give up hope. The world may forget them when they become old — they may have no one to throw a rug over them when they get cold — but God will never forget his people. Listen to these wonderful words of God to his people: 'Even to your old age, I am he, and

I hope they keep us warmer than the rabbits!

even to grey hairs I will carry you!' (Isaiah 46:4). God will never desert his people. He has promised us that. We may lose our memory altogether, but God will still take care of us. He has promised that he will never leave nor forsake his people for whom Christ died (Hebrews 13:5). This is a wonderful promise and we know that God always keeps his promises.

However, reader, you have a responsibility to the old people in your community. Maybe you have elderly parents or grandparents who need a visit at times. Don't forget them in their old age. But there are other old people in the community who have no friends and no one to really care for them. Try to make a friend of some elderly person. Go and talk to the senior citizens. You will find that they will love you for taking an interest in them. And you may even learn something from them!

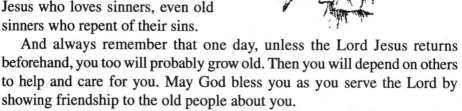

If you know some older folk who are Christians, get them to talk about what Jesus Christ has done for them. They love to think about the good things in store for them when they go to be with the Lord. If you find an old person who is not a Christian, take the opportunity of speaking to him or her about Jesus who loves sinners, even old sinners who repent of their sins.

And always remember that one day, unless the Lord Jesus returns beforehand, you too will probably grow old. Then you will depend on others to help and care for you. May God bless you as you serve the Lord by showing friendship to the old people about you.

Activities

●●

1. What are some of the problems faced by old people?
2. Name an aged person that you love and help. How do you help that person?
3. Name some special promises that God has made to old people.
4. What do you think the world will be like when you are grey-headed (that is, if you have any hair left on your head!)?

The birds will have to go!

Read
Psalm 84:1-4,10-12

'How lovely is your tabernacle, O LORD of hosts! My soul longs, yes, even faints for the courts of the LORD; my heart and my flesh cry out for the living God' (Psalm 84:1-2).

I love birds. Often Val and I sit on the verandah and watch the many brightly coloured parrots that fly into the trees near our home. They are beautiful to watch. When I see them I know that God loves colour.

When I was young I used to catch birds to keep as pets. At home on the farm I had a huge aviary in which I kept quite a number of birds.

A few years ago, when he was very small, one of my grandchildren, Scott, had a duck which used to follow him about. They were very good friends.

I can remember some funny incidents with birds. I recall Dad driving home one night in the old Ford car. There were no glass windows in the car, only windows like blinds that we pulled down. In the middle of the canvas-

 blind window there was some clear material through which we could see. One particular night a huge owl flew down from a

115

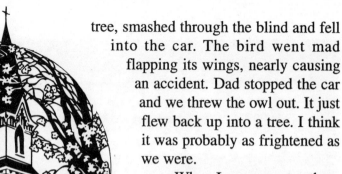

tree, smashed through the blind and fell into the car. The bird went mad flapping its wings, nearly causing an accident. Dad stopped the car and we threw the owl out. It just flew back up into a tree. I think it was probably as frightened as we were.

When I was a pastor there were trees around our church building and so we always had birds flying around. One Sunday morning during the service I noticed several people scratching their heads and necks. I thought nothing more of it and no one said anything to me. The next Sunday there were a lot of people scratching and everyone started complaining: 'Jim, there are lice in the church. There must be starlings nesting in the roof. We'll have to get rid of them.'

Now lice are found on starlings, so we had to get into the church roof, catch the starlings and put them out. We had to get rid of the nests as well. I don't know where the starlings went after they left us, but I imagine that somewhere else in town there would have been people scratching.

Now a church building is just that — a building. But it is a useful building for church folk to use for services. Christians love their church buildings because they are the homes they use with others to worship God. Each Sunday, members of my congregation would get out of bed, dress themselves for worship and with joy in their hearts set off for the church building. There we were able to worship God, no matter what the weather was like outside. The church building was a home for God's people, who are the real church. The members of the congregation had a special affection for their place of worship. It was a place of safety and security and some had been converted as they sat worshipping in that building.

In today's text we have King David's words. He was absent from the place of worship — the tent or the tabernacle. (There was no temple for worship in the days of King David; the first temple was built when his son Solomon was king.) David longed to be back with the saints to worship God.

In the tabernacle even a little sparrow had built a nest and was safe. No one was going to pull down her nest and throw her out. In the tabernacle the sparrow could safely raise her young.

But David loved the times of worship. He loved God and desired to serve him day after day. To David a day of worship was of greater value

116

and pleasure than a thousand days spent doing something else. Do you love God like that?

One of the psalms that were sung by the pilgrims who went up to Jerusalem at the times of the feasts was Psalm 122, which begins with the words: 'I was glad when they said to me, "Let us go into the house of the LORD."' Can you say these words and mean them with all your heart and soul?

David hated sin, as do all of God's people. He was not happy when he was surrounded by people who had no love for God. He always wanted to be mixing with the saints. And that must be the case with you and me if we are followers of Christ. My best friends are God's people. I don't like mixing with people who delight in sin. David's longing was to be with God. He wanted to have a place in God's eternal kingdom, even if only as the doorkeeper.

If you love Christ, then you will be able to sing those wonderful words: 'And I will dwell in the house of the LORD for ever' (Psalm 23:6). This is the hope of all God's people — to live with God in the kingdom he has prepared for his people.

If you don't enjoy worshipping with the people of God today, you have no part in his kingdom, because you would be unhappy in heaven serving Christ and living the life of holiness with all the saints. May God give you a love for himself, a love of worship and a love of mixing with his people.

Activities

● ●

1. Make a list of ten different birds found where you live.
2. What is the real meaning of 'church'?
3. Jesus Christ will one day return and take his people to be with him for ever. Talk about the place that Christ has prepared.

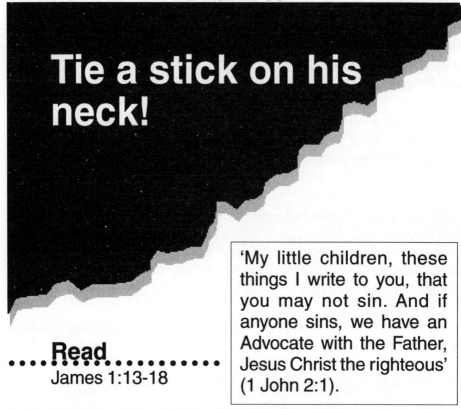

Tie a stick on his neck!

Read
James 1:13-18

'My little children, these things I write to you, that you may not sin. And if anyone sins, we have an Advocate with the Father, Jesus Christ the righteous' (1 John 2:1).

Sin is terrible because it means that the perfect law of God is broken. God is offended by our sins and has said, 'The wages of sin is death' (Romans 6:23).

All the trouble and misery that is found in this world is due to sin — Adam's sin and the sins that you and I commit day by day. We were born in sin, which means every person born into this world — except the Lord Jesus Christ — is a sinner by nature. We can't help sinning because we inherit the sinful nature of Adam.

Sadly, we love our sins. Without the Holy Spirit breaking the power of sin in our hearts, we would go on for ever sinning and loving our sins.

However, the Scriptures tell us a wonderful truth concerning the work of the Lord Jesus Christ. An angel from God appeared to Joseph and told him that Mary would give birth: 'And she will bring forth a Son, and you shall call his name Jesus, for he will save his people from their sins' (Matthew 1:21). Now what does this mean?

There are two meanings to this verse of Scripture. First of all, we are told that Jesus would die upon a cross to save his people from the punishment due to them because of their sins. But there is a second meaning which is important for all who have been saved by Jesus. We are taught in this verse that Jesus will save us from committing sins.

Christians are people who have had their nature changed. Instead of loving their sins, they hate them. Now they love God instead of wanting nothing to do with him. But Christians still sin and God begins the work of moulding repentant sinners into the likeness of Jesus Christ. Christians are being trained to avoid sin.

On the farm we used to rear calves. John and I had our favourites. After they were weaned we had to feed them. We had to teach them to drink milk out of a bucket. We would put a hand into the calf's mouth and then lower it into the bucket of milk. The calf would lower its head still sucking our fingers. As the hand dipped below the level of liquid in the bucket the calf would get the taste of the milk and it wouldn't be long before it was drinking straight from the bucket.

Now young calves have a lot of energy. They run around the paddock playing with each other and having a great time. Some of the calves were nuisances as they wouldn't stay in their own field. They looked longingly through the wire fence. They would put their heads between the wires and push through. Many times John and I would have to catch them and return them to their own paddock. Sometimes a calf would squeeze through the fence and out onto the road. One was killed by a passing car.

We had to find a way to prevent these troublesome calves from getting through fences. It was really easy to do. Dad would say, 'Get a stick and put it on that calf's neck.' John and I would then get a strong piece of thin wood and tie it on the calf's neck. When the calf tried to get through the fence all

it could do was get its head through. The stick caught against the fence wires and so the calf couldn't escape from its paddock. After a few weeks of wearing a stick on its neck the calf would have learnt not to try to get through fences. We could then take the stick off as the calf would be trained to behave itself.

At other times we would send the dog down to them. They would soon move away from the fence when they saw the dog racing towards them and growling.

Now God wants his people

to keep away from sin and to live like the Lord Jesus Christ. Satan, of course, wants Christians to go on sinning. The Holy Spirit begins the work of keeping the saints free from sin. 'How does he do this?' you may ask.

First, when we read our Bibles we discover how to live in a way that pleases God. If we love Jesus we will show that love by being obedient to God's commands. Secondly, God uses our consciences to tell us when we have sinned. You all know that secret voice in your mind that tells you when you have done wrong, don't you? We should all take notice of our consciences. And God also gives you parents, grandparents, ministers, elders, Sunday School teachers and other folk to teach you the way of God.

Of course, there are times when God has to take harsh action to bring our sinning to an end. Just as we had to send the dog down to chase the calves back from the fence — and that sometimes meant the dog would bite the calves' legs — so God sometimes has to force us to give up our sins. There are times when God causes sickness to come upon his people to remind them that they are to live a godly life. When we make an idol of something in our lives God may take it away from us. Then we can spend our time serving him.

What are we to do when we sin? Our text gives us the answer. We are to go to God through Jesus Christ our Saviour and Mediator and ask him to forgive us for the sake of his Son Jesus. If our repentance is sincere then we are truly forgiven.

Today's reading teaches us that we are to control our desires and so avoid sin. This means we must control the thoughts of our minds and hearts.

There is nothing wrong with looking at a toy and thinking it is wonderful. But you must then be careful that your mind does not begin to say, 'I want that toy. I'll steal it.' If you start thinking along those lines, then you must get away from the toy and do something else because there is a danger that you may try to steal it. If that happens the sin which began in your mind will have become fully grown and James tells us that such sin 'brings forth death' (James 1:15).

Christian friend, keep your eyes on Jesus and live a life of obedience to him.

Activities

● ●

1. Read your text carefully. What is an 'advocate'?
2. What does the name 'Jesus' mean?
3. How does God want us to live?
4. Name something that could become an idol in your life.

Stop complaining!

Read
• • • • • • • • • • • • • • • •
2 Corinthians 12:1-10

'And we know that all things work together for good to those who love God, to those who are the called according to his purpose' (Romans 8:28).

Throughout our lives things happen to us and we wonder why. We sometimes ask, 'Why is God letting this happen to me?' And so often we have no answer. But God is all-wise and knows exactly what he is doing. This thought should comfort us in the difficult times.

I found that I needed back surgery and the result was that I had to resign from the ministry. The surgery didn't do what it was supposed to do. I didn't ask God, 'Why should this happen to *me*?' I know that, because of sin, sickness and death strike each one of us. But the question I kept asking God at first was: 'Lord, what is the reason for what is happening? It's not just me that is being hurt but also my congregation.'

I don't know the answer to that question. However, as I know that God only does what is right I can have peace of mind. Of course, I could start complaining to God, but that would only make my life miserable — as well as Valerie's life and that of others close to me. Christians shouldn't be grumblers. We might not be overjoyed by our hard times, but we should not complain about God's providence.

Many years ago my wife was involved in teaching children water safety. Each summer the Education Department in our area employed six or seven

teachers to take groups of children and teach them to swim. I always thought the teachers involved had it easy! They spent hot days in the cool water at the swimming pool. But some of the children were always complaining. They would arrive and start grumbling that it was too hot to be out in the sun. At other times they would claim that the wind or the water was too cold.

On one particular day several of the children complained about the water in the swimming pool: 'Sir, the water is stinging our eyes.' Then they spoke to my wife about the same problem. She told them to stop grizzling and to get on with their swimming. They then went to a third teacher, hoping to get some sympathy.

'Sir, the water is stinging our eyes,' they grumbled.

Now this third teacher was a lovely Christian man. He looked at the complainers and said quietly, 'You're fortunate to have eyes that sting.'

With that he put his hand to one of his eyes, pulled it out and showed it to the boys who were grumbling. My wife saw this happen and told me that the lads backed away with terrified looks on their faces. They couldn't believe that one of the teacher's eyes was sitting in his hand. They stopped complaining and finally settled down to swimming. The teacher then put his artificial eye back in place and continued instructing the children.

We asked the teacher how he lost his eye. He told the story of his schooldays when pens with sharp nibs were used for writing. I can remember making darts out of the pen-nibs. Someone had thrown a nib dart which struck him in the eye. The eye had to be removed. From that day onward Jack had a glass eye.

The apostle Paul was a faithful servant of the Lord Jesus Christ. He travelled the known world preaching the gospel. But he had a problem which he called 'a thorn in the flesh' (2 Corinthians 12:7). I think Paul suffered from eye trouble (see Galatians 4:15). Whatever it was, it was a real problem to him. In our reading we find that he pleaded three times with the Lord to heal him of his difficulty. Three times the Lord replied, 'My grace is sufficient for you, for my strength is made perfect in weakness' (v. 9).

Because of Paul's disfigurement he was not attractive to people. Yet when he preached the gospel, the power of God accompanied his preaching and people were saved. Paul had no reason for pride, because he knew that if anyone was saved it was not because he or she was such a nice person, but due to God's great power and mercy.

Thus Paul could write the words of our text: 'And we know that all things work together for good to those who love God, to those who are the called according to his purpose.' My bad back, Paul's 'thorn in the flesh', the disappointments that come to every Christian — each has a purpose in God's plan. All of our trials are for our good. We may not see the purpose now, but one day we shall understand how wise our God was in bringing hardship upon us.

Maybe part of the purpose for my bad back and forced retirement was so that I could spend time writing these stories that teach biblical truths. But I know that I can trust my God's word when he tells me that all things are working together for my good and his glory.

Isn't it wonderful that we have such a loving, all-wise God, who only does those things that bring glory to himself and good to his people? We don't have to be people who complain. We must resign our lot to the God of mercy who will never let us down. Praise God!

Activities

● ●

1. Why should Christians accept whatever happens to them without complaining?
2. What do you think Paul's 'thorn in the flesh' was?
3. How are we able to cope with all the difficulties we face during our lives?

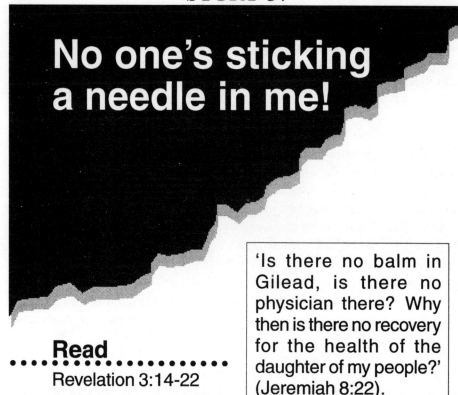

No one's sticking a needle in me!

Read
•••••••••••••••••
Revelation 3:14-22

'Is there no balm in Gilead, is there no physician there? Why then is there no recovery for the health of the daughter of my people?' (Jeremiah 8:22).

Some medical treatments hurt. Recently Aimee, one of my granddaughters, had to visit the doctor's surgery for her vaccination shots before she started school. Her father and the doctor had to hold her while the doctor did his work. All the time she yelled as she struggled to escape.

Medical treatment is often needed to help a person recover from an existing illness. Doctors are very important people to all of us. As we get older we seem to need the doctor more than ever before.

I would like to tell you about a boy who, with the other members of his family, came into contact with a man who had hepatitis, a serious illness which is very infectious. The mother rang the doctor and explained the situation. He suggested that they all visit his surgery and have an injection to prevent the family members from developing the disease.

That afternoon the family made its way to the doctor's surgery. First of all, Mum went in to see the doctor with her two daughters. Each received a needle in the buttocks. When they returned to the waiting-room Catriona came out rubbing her bottom. She made out that she was crying and complained, 'It hurts terribly!'

'Come on, Doug,' said Dad. 'It's our turn now.'

In the surgery they found the doctor getting the needles ready for the next two injections.

'Who's first?' asked the doctor.

Doug looked at his father and said, 'You can go first, Dad.'

Dad then was told to lie down on the doctor's couch. Doug saw his father wince with pain as the needle pierced his flesh.

'Your turn, Doug,' the doctor said as he pointed to the couch.

There was a sign of real terror in Doug's eyes as he looked at the needle in the doctor's hand. He took one look at the doctor and shouted, 'No one's sticking a needle in me!'

Dad had no chance of catching Doug as he raced towards the surgery door. Dad was still hitching up his trousers as Doug reached the door, pulled it open, raced through the waiting-room, past his waiting mother and sisters, and headed for the street outside.

Then Dad and the doctor appeared. The doctor spoke quite seriously: 'It's most important that Doug has his injection. Hepatitis is very contagious. Get him to come back. I'll wait here for you.'

So Dad walked out into the street and there about thirty metres down the road was Doug looking back to see what would happen. As there were quite a few people in the street Dad was embarrassed to have to call out after his runaway son. 'Doug, come here at once,' he pleaded.

Then as Dad started to walk towards him Doug began to move further away down the street. Poor old Dad didn't feel like running down the street after Doug with so many people about. Every time Dad made a move, Doug kept thirty or forty metres in front of him.

Eventually Dad had to go back to the surgery and tell the doctor that he couldn't catch Doug. The doctor, who was a friend of the family, said, 'Well I can't stay here any longer. He'll just have to take his chances with the disease.'

The family came out of the waiting-room and there was Doug still about thirty metres in front of them. Dad called out, 'Doug, we're going to the car. Be there to meet us.'

Doug then realized he had won the battle and by the time the family reached their parked car he was there too. Dad opened the doors and everyone took their seats. No one spoke for quite a time. Then as their home came into view — they lived out in the country — Dad turned his head slightly towards Doug and said sternly, 'When we get home you'll discover what happens when you disobey me!'

Doug knew Dad meant what he said. As soon as the car stopped, Dad stepped out of the car, opened the door and said to Doug, 'Get out here, son!'

Doug got out of the car with a frightened look in his eyes, ducked under Dad's hand and raced for the bush.

'Come back here, young man!' Dad shouted. But Doug put a lot of space between himself and his father. 'When I catch you, young man,' shouted his father, 'you'll never disobey me again!'

I'll leave the rest of the story up to your imagination. Doug eventually returned home for his meeting with his father. I taught Doug. It was his father who told me the story. Doug didn't want to talk about the incident at all when he came to school.

It is a silly thing to refuse medical treatment when it is available and yet when it comes to spiritual things that is what so many people do. Do you realize that we all suffer from a terrible disease called sin? There is a cure available to rid you of that disease, and that remedy is the blood of the Lord Jesus Christ. The Scriptures tell us plainly: 'The blood of Jesus Christ his Son cleanses us from all sin' (1 John 1:7).

The city of Gilead was well known for balm — an ointment that aided healing — yet many people couldn't be bothered to go and get the treatment. As a result their recovery took a lot longer, and some actually died because they refused treatment. The church at Laodicea was spiritually sick and needed spiritual medicine, though they thought they were fit and well.

Friends, there is a treatment freely available for all who are sinners. But to benefit from it they must go to the heavenly Doctor, pleading the saving work of Christ and asking to be cleansed from their sin. They can run away if they like, but the end will be eternal death — hell!

Pray that the Holy Spirit will apply to you the saving work of Christ. Then live by faith in Jesus Christ and you will live eternally in the new heavens and new earth that God will create for his people. Trust your salvation to the only one who can save, Jesus Christ. He alone is the God-given treatment for sin!

Activities

■■■

1. Find the town of Gilead in an atlas.
2. What is meant by the word 'balm'?
3. How does Jesus save his people from their sins?
4. What do you think is meant by the expression: 'The road to hell is paved with good intentions'?

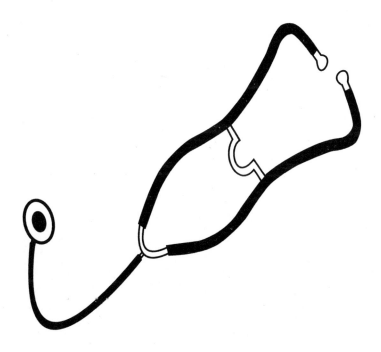

Oh, the pain!

Read
Hebrews 2:14-18;
4:14-16

'Let us therefore come boldly to the throne of grace, that we may obtain mercy and find grace to help in time of need' (Hebrews 4:16).

I wonder how many times we have gone to someone who has been suffering and said, 'I'm so sorry for you. I know what you are going through.' Yet in most cases we really have no idea how that person is feeling. And that is simply because we haven't suffered in the same way. We can use our imagination and try to imagine what someone else is going through, but we can't get inside the person's brain to really know what is going on inside his or her suffering body.

Solomon wrote a proverb about this very truth. He said, 'The heart knows its own bitterness, and a stranger does not share its joy' (Proverbs 14:10).

Today's reading tells us about our great High Priest Jesus Christ who has a true understanding of the difficulties and disappointments we suffer during our lives. That is why we can go to him in prayer, pour out our hearts and know that he understands what we are saying. He suffered greatly during his life on earth and knows what we are going through in the difficult times.

Some time ago I suffered from kidney stones. I was about 100 kilometres (sixty miles or so) from our home, driving along a country road to visit a church family, when I suddenly felt a terrible, burning pain in my lower back and under my ribs. I stopped the car, wondering what was happening to me. I thought I might be having a heart attack. I decided that in that case I should get back home as quickly as I could, so I turned the car around and headed for home. I was in the most terrible pain with perspiration pouring down my face. My heart was beating very quickly as I drove along.

Eventually I pulled up at the bottom of the steps to our house and was met by Valerie who asked, 'Whatever is wrong? You look as white as a sheet.'

I replied, 'Don't say anything. I just need to lie down. Ring the doctor. I'm in terrible pain.'

It wasn't long before I was at the doctor's surgery, tests were done and a kidney stone was diagnosed. I was given a pain-killing injection and told to visit a specialist who dealt with my particular problem.

I returned from the doctor still in a lot of pain and Valerie was very sympathetic. 'I know you must be suffering terribly,' she said soothingly. 'Come and lie down on the bed and rest easily. Maybe the injection will ease the pain and you can get to sleep.'

'Valerie, you have no idea how I feel,' I replied. 'No one can understand the pain I'm suffering.' Then I walked into the lounge and lay on my side on the floor with my knees pulled up under my chin.

'That can't be comfortable,' Valerie said. 'Come and stretch out on the bed. You'll feel much better.'

I said I was staying just where I was as that position seemed the most comfortable. And there I stayed until the effects of the injection began to ease the pain. Then I staggered into the bedroom and lay down.

A day or so later I was in hospital having a kidney stone removed.

Many people met me later and said, 'I know just how you must have felt.'

Whenever anyone said that I would ask, 'Have you ever had a kidney stone?' When they replied, 'No,' I told them they had no real idea how I felt. I know they were being sympathetic, but if you have never had a kidney stone you have no idea of the pain involved. I had five kidney stones over the four years that followed, each requiring treatment in hospital.

After this had happened a couple of times, Valerie came to me one evening and said, 'I've a terrible pain in my side. I need to see the doctor at once.' From the description of her pain I thought that maybe she had a kidney stone. The doctor confirmed this to be true. And from that day onwards, Valerie fully understood what I suffered when my kidney stones began to move. She even suggested that I should lie on the floor and pull my legs up under my chin. She had done the same and found it a comfortable position for someone suffering from kidney stones. It is only when we have suffered in the same way as other people that we can truly understand what they are going through.

Today's reading tells us that Christ was truly man as well as God. He experienced so much of what we go through — and that to a greater extent than we can ever imagine. He did not know what it was to sin, as he was sinless, but he was tempted. He experienced pain and death and knew what it was like to be deserted by those who were his friends. As our sin-bearer he endured the anger of God.

This is a wonderful truth for all who love their Saviour: Jesus knows how you feel because he has experienced what you are going through. So we are commanded to approach Christ in prayer humbly but with confidence. When you pray, tell Jesus all about your joys and pains. Ask him to provide an answer to what you are going through. And all the time remember that he understands what you are saying, because, with the exception of sin, he has experienced everything that you do.

What a wonderful Advocate we have in heaven today — Jesus Christ, the Son of God! He hears our prayers and presents them to his Father on our behalf. What a wonderful Saviour!

Activities

● ●

1. Why is it that Jesus is able to understand what we are saying in our prayers?
2. When we are in difficulties to whom do we go for help?
3. Who is the Christian's great High Priest? What is the work of a priest?

This job will take for ever!

.... Read ....
Matthew 25:31-46

> 'And these will go away into everlasting punishment, but the righteous into eternal life' (Matthew 25:46).

The words 'everlasting'and 'eternal' are found scattered throughout the Bible. It is very difficult to understand what these words mean. When we repent of our sins and trust in Christ for salvation, eternal life is ours then and there. All those who live for themselves and have no interest in Christ are under God's condemnation and unless they repent and come to Christ their punishment will be hell — everlasting banishment from the presence of God.

I sometimes look up into the night sky and think about space going on without an end. My mind understands the words, but I cannot take in what they really mean.

To be in the presence of Christ eternally is a wonderful thing. To be cast into hell for all eternity is something to be greatly feared. But what really is eternity?

When I was principal of a city school we had a continual problem with vandals breaking in. Again and again we would arrive at school to find that valuable equipment had been stolen. On other occasions those involved in breaking into the school threw things about and generally made a mess.

On one occasion the colour television set in my office was stolen as well as the keys to all the doors. Every lock had to be replaced and that was a

costly business. That same night, the thieves broke into the library and threw books and other material about. When the librarian arrived at school she was very upset about the damage. I left her to look things over and asked her to let me know what help she needed to get the library working again. Half an hour later she came into my office with tears in her eyes. She said that it would take a little time to get the books back on the shelves. Not many had been damaged and for this she was very grateful. However, the reason she was crying was because tens of thousands of catalogue cards had been tipped out of the filing cabinets and scattered about on the floor.

The librarian looked at me and said, 'This job will take for ever! I'll need a lot of help to sort out the cards.' When I had a look at the cards scattered all over the floor I was very pleased I was not the librarian. I knew that the sorting out would be a slow, tedious job. But it had to be done and with the help of some kind parents, a couple of weeks later all the catalogue cards were back in their correct order in the filing cabinets.

That job eventually came to an end, but the term 'for ever' means never-ending. Just imagine if there had been a million cards scattered about on the floor. The sorting out would probably have taken years. But even then it would have come to an end one day. But if something is really for ever it never comes to an end.

All of us who are Christians should rejoice that the life we have with Christ is eternal. This means we shall be in the presence of the Lord Jesus Christ for a period that will never end. We shall always inhabit the perfect kingdom that he has prepared for his people. This thought should fill our hearts with joy.

132

But if you have no saving faith in Jesus Christ your destiny is eternal hell. That will mean your situation is really hopeless. Never will you escape the clutches of hell. What a terrible thought! The very worst things that happen on earth all eventually come to an end — even if the end comes about through death. But not so eternal hell. The inhabitants of hell can never escape.

Friend, consider what the Scriptures tell you about eternity. I pray that you will be one of those who will spend eternity with the Saviour, Jesus Christ, and that none of my readers will have a part in the place of everlasting punishment. If you have not already done so, run to Christ now for salvation!

Activities

● ●

1. What is meant by 'everlasting punishment'?
2. What is 'eternal life'?
3. How do sinners gain eternal life?

I'll have my money, thank you!

'You shall not covet your neighbour's house; you shall not covet your neighbour's wife, nor his manservant, nor his maidservant, nor his ox, nor his donkey, nor anything that is your neighbour's' (Exodus 20:17).

Read
Luke 12:13-21

So many sins start in the mind. Sinners think about things and too often the thought ends up by coming to pass (James 1:12-15). The covetous person is someone who has seen something and then wants it for himself. He spends time thinking about the object and in many cases he ends up making an idol of it in his mind.

The Lord clearly warns us that covetous thoughts are sinful. We are to be satisfied with our lot in life and never steal what does not belong to us. This doesn't mean that we are not to work to better ourselves. But whatever we do must be done in a moral way and one that glorifies God. Many people covet the things of the world. Maybe today we don't spend our time coveting our neighbour's donkey, but we may be guilty of coveting our friend's bicycle, car, or other possessions.

Coveting is a terrible sin, resulting in the loss of eternal life if there is no repentance. Read the story of the young man who went to Jesus and asked him the question: 'Good Teacher, what good thing shall I do that I may have eternal life?' (Matthew 19:16). This young man had made a god of his wealth. He turned away from Christ and went his way. He loved his possessions more than he loved eternal life. He coveted the things of the world and wanted more and more. So coveting can bring great losses.

One day, Valerie and I were having a picnic beside the sea when several magpies came and perched in the trees nearby looking down at us as we ate our meal. We occasionally threw a scrap of bread and watched the magpies fighting over it.

Then Valerie and I each threw a piece of crust to the birds. Mine was a small crust while Valerie was much more generous. Down flew the magpies, each with its eyes fixed on the piece it wanted. The bravest bird came close to us and grabbed the small crust. He was just about to fly away when he spied the larger crust. The other magpie was very timid and at first kept away.

The more daring magpie then dropped his small crust. He could see the bigger crust and that was the piece he now wanted. The timid magpie quickly grabbed the small crust he had dropped and gobbled it down. Then, before the other magpie could get the big crust he coveted, a third magpie flew down out of a tree, grabbed it in his beak and flew off. The courageous but greedy magpie had lost everything.

Today's reading is about a man who loved his possessions. He lived for them. He built bigger barns to store them in. But he lost everything. He died and was called into God's presence for judgement. All he had worked for during his life was left behind. But the tragedy of the story was that the rich man was not spiritually rich. In our reading Jesus plainly says, 'Take heed and beware of covetousness, for one's life does not consist in the abundance of the things he possesses' (Luke 12:15).

We must make sure that we keep our eyes on our own property and do not covet things that belong to other people. In fact we need to get our eyes off the things of the world altogether and onto Jesus. When a person is born of God's Spirit he or she has the victory. The apostle John wrote, 'For whatever is born of God overcomes the world. And this is the victory that has overcome the world — our faith' (1 John 5:4).

Reader, don't spend your time loving the things of the world. Rather seek to be filled with love for Jesus.

Activities

● ●

1. What does the word 'covet' mean?
2. What are some of the things people covet today?
3. If you see something you would like to own, how do you deal with the problem?

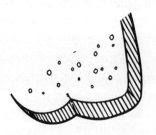

The arch met in the middle

Read
....
John 14:12-18

'For there is one God and one Mediator between God and men, the Man Christ Jesus' (1 Timothy 2:5).

In the course of our lives there are many times we need someone to act on our behalf. When I purchased a piece of land I needed a solicitor to act on my behalf. He was the middle man between myself and the government department that registered the land purchase in my name. The solicitor was a man I knew. He knew what I wanted and I could understand what he was saying. He also understood the legal language needed for dealing with the government department.

When I first saw Valerie, my future wife, standing on a railway station ready to catch a train for teachers' college I asked a friend, 'Who's that girl over there?' She knew Valerie, so I asked, 'How about introducing me to her? She looks like a nice girl.' The go-between duly did the introductions, and four years later we were married. Middle men — or in this case a middle woman — are very handy people!

When the Sydney Harbour Bridge was built in the 1930s the construction commenced from each side of the harbour. The plan was to have the bridge meet in the middle and then traffic could easily cross the expanse of water. Very careful planning was required as the builders would have been very embarrassed if the two sections did not meet exactly. But the careful planning resulted in the archway joining just as planned. Even so, I read that the bolt

that was to drop through the two overlapping holes would not fit until the heat of the sun had expanded the steel slightly. Then it dropped into place and all was well. Now the two sides of the harbour were joined and people could easily cross over the roadway suspended from the arch. In some ways the Sydney Harbour Bridge acts like a mediator. It is the go-between, joining the two sides of the harbour.

Now sinners have a real problem and it is this: 'How can a sinful person have any contact with a holy God?' Or we could put the question the other way round and ask, 'How can a holy God have contact with a sinful person?' Sin in the Garden of Eden destroyed the fellowship between God and man. So it was that a go-between who could re-establish fellowship between God and man had to be found.

Jesus Christ is the only one who can act as mediator between God and man. Jesus is both God and man in one person. As man he can represent humans in the presence of God for two reasons: first, because he is without sin; secondly, because he is God he can approach God on our behalf.

I have written elswhere about the fact that Jesus Christ was our representative and substitute on earth, bearing our sins and living the life of perfect obedience to his Father. He has won salvation for his people. But how can I, a sinful person, approach our pure and perfectly holy God? I cannot do so myself. I need the Mediator, Jesus Christ. So when I pray to my heavenly Father I do so in the name of Jesus, my Mediator. It is Jesus who presents my prayers to God and who gains God's blessings for me. It is Jesus Christ who makes intercession for his people.

The apostle Paul put it like this: 'It is Christ who died, and furthermore is also risen, who is even at the right hand of God, who also makes intercession for us' (Romans 8:34). This very day, Jesus Christ is in heaven representing his people before the throne of God. All the blessings we receive are due to the work of our Mediator, Jesus Christ. All of our worship of God is made acceptable because of what he has done on our behalf.

The saints in heaven are not mediators between God and men, because they are not God and man in the one person. Mary, the mother of Jesus, is not a mediator. She was a godly young woman chosen by God to be the mother of Jesus. Never let anyone tell you that there are any mediators between God and humans other than the Lord Jesus Christ. Remember the words of the text for today: 'There is one God and one Mediator between God and men, the Man Christ Jesus.'

Jesus understands your needs, so go to him in prayer. Then give thanks to God through Jesus for all the wonderful blessings you receive.

Activities

• •

1. What is a mediator?
2. What important work is Jesus doing in heaven today?
3. What is the significance of the expression that Jesus is 'at the right hand of God'?
4. Where is heaven?

I love my boat

Read
Ecclesiastes 5:10-17

'Do not love the world or the things in the world. If anyone loves the world, the love of the Father is not in him' (1 John 2:15).

A person I know very well has a saying which she uses now and again. When her husband sees something he could use he usually discusses the matter with her. He asks if buying the object would be a wise decision. She often replies, 'Go and get it now and make use of it. Everything will be burned up one day.'

There is no doubt that for many people the things of the world are most attractive. In the Western world we have so much of everything. On the whole, life is easy, we have plenty of everything and we enjoy living for the things of the world. Even Christians can fall into the trap of putting the things of the world before the things of God.

God has given us a wonderful world to enjoy. We should make sensible use of God's gifts, but always remember that one day we shall die and all that we own will be left behind. Job put it this way: 'Naked I came from my mother's womb, and naked I shall return there' (Job 1:21).

When we go to a funeral we don't see a removal van carrying the dead person's belongings following along after the hearse. Everything that the dead person used to own now belongs to someone else. None of us can take our possessions with us when we die.

To love the things of the world more than the things of God is a sad situation for any person to be in. God must be first in everything. I have things that I care for greatly. My wife and family are very important to me. Even my Apple Macintosh computer is precious to me. My library of books I treat with great care, but I know that the day is coming when I must say, 'Goodbye,' to all of the things I hold precious. The more we love the things of the world, the harder it will be to die. So let us all hold the things of the world very lightly.

I heard the story of a husband and wife who went to church one night and there they heard a very fine sermon concerning the return of the Lord Jesus Christ. The wife was bubbling over with excitement when they arrived home.

'Won't it be wonderful to see Jesus returning in power and glory?' she said to her husband.

Her husband didn't sound so enthusiastic but replied, 'I suppose so.'

When they sat down to have a cup of tea before going to bed the wife said to her husband, 'Trevor, you don't seem to be very excited about the return of the Lord. Wouldn't it be wonderful if he returned tonight and took us into the new creation to enjoy him for ever?'

But Trevor, who had just purchased a new boat for fishing, looked at his wife and replied in a quiet voice: 'Well, I'm looking forward to the return of Christ, but I don't want him to come for a while.'

'Why ever not?' asked Verity, his wife.

'Because I want a few months to enjoy my new boat. I've only just bought it,' Trevor replied.

Now I don't know if this is a true story or not, but there are some people who love the things of the world so much that they hate the thought of the return of Christ because it will mean that all the things they love so much will be no more. And people who love the things of the world never seem to be satisfied. Our reading for today tells us this truth. Many people just want more and more.

Our reading also reminds us that valuable possessions can cause great concern. A little while ago a number of houses in our area were broken into and valuables stolen. This caused all of us who lived there to be concerned about our possessions and how to protect them from thieves.

As we have already seen, our reading also teaches that we can take nothing with us in death. The only treasure that counts when we die is the spiritual treasure that is stored up for us in heaven.

The Christian should be someone who looks forward to the coming of Christ because it means leaving this world of sin and death and going to be with Jesus, the giver of eternal life and pure joy.

Reader, take to heart the words of the Lord Jesus Christ who said, 'Do not lay up for yourselves treasures on earth, where moth and rust destroy and where thieves break in and steal; but lay up for yourselves treasures in heaven, where neither moth nor rust destroys and where thieves do not break in and steal. For where your treasure is, there your heart will be also' (Matthew 6:19-21).Where is your heart?

Activities

● ●

1. What will happen to this world when Jesus Christ returns?
2. Is it sinful to enjoy the world God has created for humans?
3. What does the apostle John mean when he tells us that we are not to 'love the world or the things in the world'?
4. What do you love more than anything else in the world?

Where's that bird?

‘Can the blind lead the blind? Will they not both fall into the ditch?’ (Luke 6:39).

....Read.............
Ezekiel 33:1-9

Everywhere you go there are warning signs. They are put up to tell people of danger. When travelling in several Asian countries we saw signs warning travellers of the dangers of carrying prohibited drugs. The notices usually concluded with a warning that the death penalty would be the result of a guilty verdict. When we travel about our cities there are signs telling us when and where we can cross the road. Car drivers are confronted with 'Stop' signs, 'Go slow' signs, 'Give way' signs, speed limit signs, and so on.

Slippery Road

Wherever there are warning signs, they are usually very clearly written and many are printed in red. This means that people cannot help seeing them. They have no excuse if something goes wrong. But some signals are not very clear.

One day my wife and I visited a lady who was a member of our congregation. During our stay every now and again I heard what I thought was a bird chirping. I kept looking around the room as the bird seemed so very close. The lady saw my puzzled look and said, 'You can hear the bird too? I think it must be trapped in the ceiling of the house. It's been squawking now for a couple of days.'

I went outside and had a look all round the house, but there didn't seem to be anywhere that a bird could get into the ceiling. When we left I told the lady that I was sure the bird would find its way out and the squawking would stop. On the way home Valerie and I wondered how a bird could have found its way under the roof of the house.

That evening Valerie called me into the lounge and said, 'I can't believe this, but I can hear a bird squeaking in our ceiling. It's just like the one we heard this morning.'

I listened and, sure enough, every now and again I too could hear a bird chirping. I climbed through the trapdoor in the ceiling and into the roof, but couldn't see any bird. In fact I couldn't hear one up there. During the night I heard the bird squawking every now and again.

The next morning I rang the lady we had visited and asked, 'Do you still have your little bird?'

'Yes, it's still here,' she replied.

'Well, it's amazing,' I said. 'We have one too. I wonder what's going on?'

Our bird squawked all afternoon on a very regular basis. Valerie and I were getting sick of it and wondered what we should do. Then the phone rang and one of the more thinking members of my congregation spoke to me. In passing I told him about the bird that seemed to be trapped in our ceiling. He was silent for a while and then burst out laughing.

'I can hear it,' he said through much laughter.

'What's so funny?' I asked.

'Do you have a smoke detector in the room?' he asked.

'Yes,' I replied.

'Your bird is the smoke detector,' he said, still laughing. 'Didn't you read the instructions when you put it up? The noise is to let you know that the battery is almost flat and needs replacing.'

I could hardly believe what he told me. 'Just a minute,' I said, 'I'll check it out.' No sooner had I removed the battery than the bird noise stopped. The warning signal had meant nothing to me. Every time I think of the incident I feel silly. I should have known.

Our reading today tells us that Ezekiel was appointed as God's watchman over Israel. His job was to warn the people, in a language they could clearly understand, that God's judgement was about to fall on them. If they took notice of what he said they would save their lives. If not, then they would die. But Ezekiel had to give God's warning to the people, whether or not they paid attention.

Jesus spoke of spiritually blind leaders who failed to warn the people of God's anger towards unrepentant sinners. Those leaders were spiritually blind, as were the people they led. Neither knew where they were going, so they all ended up in a ditch — in other words, they didn't escape the judgement of God.

Today God warns us in the Bible, through the preaching of the Word, the witness of his people and other ways known to you all. All must take notice of God's warnings. We need to read his Word and obey his commands. If we don't read the Bible's instructions we shall never know God's warnings.

Read your Bible, listen to all the witnessing of God's people and take heed of what is said. Make sure you attend a church where the pastor is not one who is spiritually blind, but rather is a man who points you to the only Saviour, Jesus Christ. Ask God to direct your path to Christ, where you will find eternal life.

Activities

• •

1. Who was Christ speaking about when he said, 'The blind lead the blind'?
2. Who was Ezekiel?
3. What warning did Ezekiel give the people of Israel?
4. How can you tell if your pastor is teaching the truth?

Dig up that tree!

> 'And if it bears fruit, well. But if not, after that you can cut it down' (Luke 13:9).

..... Read ....
Isaiah 5:1-7

We have some lovely shrubs and trees growing in our small garden. Both Valerie and I enjoy looking at the trees and the colourful flowers they bear at different times of the year. We are always looking out for something different that we can plant.

Some time ago we read an article and saw very colourful photographs about the Powton tree, or the Chinese Dragon tree. The article claimed that the tree grew one metre in its first year and three metres during its second year. It was a deciduous tree which produced long spikes of flowers each springtime.

We thought that such a tree would be great in our garden. We found a nursery that sold the Powton tree and soon had it growing. It certainly grew a metre in the first year and the first spring saw a dozen or so flowers on its three branches. Valerie and I thought this was a good start to our exotic tree. With plenty of fertilizer and water the tree grew furiously during the

146

second year. We had great expectations of many spikes of flowers, but again there were only a dozen or so small flowers.

I was becoming disappointed with the tree and spoke to it quite severely.

I warned it that it would be dug out next spring if it didn't produce a good crop of flowers! Again it was well watered and given the very best fertilizer. But the flowers didn't appear at springtime so I dug it out and replaced it with another flowering tree.

Today's reading tells of a vineyard planted and cared for by God. That vineyard was God's covenant people of Israel. They were precious to the Lord and he cared for them as a farmer would care for his vineyard. But the nation, despite the attention paid to them, failed to produce the fruit that was expected. The Israelites were to produce holiness in their lives. They were expected to glorify their God and tell the surrounding nations of the wonder of Jehovah. But they failed in their God-given task. They produced no fruit. So we read the words of God concerning his vineyard:

> I will lay it waste;
> It shall not be pruned or dug,
> But there shall come up briers and thorns.
> I will also command the clouds
> That they rain no more on it
>
> (Isaiah 5:6).

God cast off his rebellious people after they had crucified the Lord Jesus.

Our text for today contains the same message: produce spiritual fruit, or be cut down and cast out. In the parable a fig-tree is mentioned. It was not producing the expected fruit and so the instruction was given to the gardener: 'Look after the tree. If it bears fruit, good and well. If not, then cut it down.' We are not told if the tree was kept or cut down, but the warning was clear.

The people of Israel were warned: 'Serve the Lord and produce the fruit of holiness, or you will be destroyed.' But there is also a message here to all who profess faith in Jesus Christ. The message simply is: if you say you are a Christian, then live like one; produce the fruit of righteousness and godliness. Make sure you are producing the fruit of the Spirit in your daily life. If not, then God, through his Word, will call you to repentance.

He will send teachers and pastors to encourage you and direct your ways. But if you do not take notice of what is expected of you, then get ready for cutting down.

God may well leave you in your sins and harden your heart so that you cannot receive the gospel. He may put you in a place where you no longer have godly pastors calling you to repentance. You may be left alone till the Day of Judgement, when you will be cut down and cast into the eternal fires of hell. The warning is plain! Repent of your sins and faithfully follow Christ, producing the fruit of repentance. If you do this you will live. If not, then be ready to face an angry God.

The teaching of today's passage of Scripture can be summed up in these words:

Seek the LORD while he may be found,
Call upon him while he is near.
Let the wicked forsake his way,
And the unrighteous man his thoughts;
Let him return to the LORD,
And he will have mercy on him;
And to our God,
For he will abundantly pardon

(Isaiah 55:6-7).

May God be pleased to bless all who read these words.

Activities

●●

1. What is a vineyard?
2. What fruit must a Christian produce in his or her life?
3. What is the 'fruit of the Spirit'?

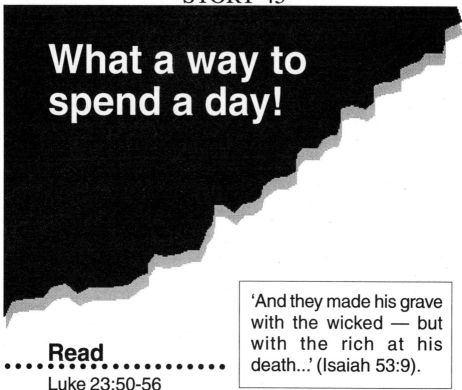

What a way to spend a day!

Read

Luke 23:50-56

'And they made his grave with the wicked — but with the rich at his death...' (Isaiah 53:9).

Graveyards can be very interesting places to wander through. There is much history engraved on the headstones that mark places of burial.

One family in my congregation were deeply involved in tracing their family tree. They spent a lot of time and money reading about their ancestors and obtaining copies of birth, marriage and death certificates. They also spent many hours seeking out the places where their ancestors were buried.

They had a family and sometimes the children would complain, 'Mum, Dad, why do we have to spend so many Saturdays walking through cemeteries?' The children had many a picnic sitting beside graves. Many long days were spent in old cemeteries. But eventually the family tree was completed and graveyards were no longer used as picnic spots.

I'm not too interested in family trees. I have some information about my ancestors, but that was sorted out by someone else. And I'm not really interested in looking at headstones in cemeteries. But one day a friend asked me if I had ever seen the place where the first Cromarty settler in Australia was buried. I hadn't, so our family visited a cemetery out in the bush not far from the sea. I'm pleased I visited that spot because it reminded me that many of my ancestors were Christians.

The headstone had the appropriate heading and name, followed by an account of the death of Captain William Cromarty and his sixteen-year-old son. It read:

HERE ARE BURIED
SUCH REMAINS AS WERE FOUND
OF THE BODIES OF
CAPT. WILLIAM CROMARTY, AGED 50 YEARS
AND
WILLIAM HIS SON, AGED 16 YEARS
WHO HAVING LEFT THEIR HOMES ON THE MORNING
OF SEPTEMBER THE 1ST, 1838. ACCOMPANIED BY
AN ASSIGNED MAN SERVANT, AND AN ABORIGINAL
NATIVE, FOR THE PURPOSE OF RECOVERING A BOAT
WHICH HAD BEEN CAST ASHORE AT THE HEADS,
WERE NO MORE SEEN, HAVING PERISHED, IT IS
SUPPOSED IN LAUNCHING IT THROUGH THE SURF.

READER! LET THIS ADMONISH THEE OF THE UNCERTAINTY
OF THE PRESENT LIFE; AND MAY GOD'S HOLY SPIRIT
TEACH THEE SO TO LIVE THAT DEATH MAY NEVER FIND
THEE UNPREPARED!

...William and his son aged 16 years
who having left their homes
on the morning of September the 1st, 1838,
accompanied by an assigned man servant,
and an aboriginal native
for the purpose of recovering a boat
which had been cast ashore at the heads,
were no more seen, having perished, it is supposed,
in launching it through the surf.

This was then followed by the words:

Reader! Let this admonish thee
of the uncertainty of the present life;
and may God's Holy Spirit teach thee so to live
that death may never find thee unprepared!

Headstones today don't usually have too many words, but looking at the words engraved on them, especially old ones, can be interesting.

Today's text was a prophecy concerning the death and burial of the Lord Jesus Christ. The reading tells you about the fulfilment of that prophecy. When our Saviour was crucified he was the bearer of the sins of his people. His death was with the wicked. He was crucified with thieves on either side of him. The people who stood around the crosses that day thought Jesus was just another criminal getting his just deserts. They mocked him and the majority of those present were pleased to see him die.

Jesus 'made his grave with the wicked...' This was the final act in the humiliation of our Saviour. But just before Christ died he shouted out, 'It is finished!' (John 19:30). Those words were a cry of victory. Jesus was not simply saying that his life was over — finished — but rather that the great work of saving his people was now finished. In other words, he was saying, 'The work is accomplished!' Jesus had done the work that his Father had given him to do. He had paid the penalty for the sins of his people. It was then, and only then, that he could dismiss his spirit.

Normally when people were crucified, their bodies were thrown onto the rubbish heap, unless some friend or relative paid to get the body back, in which case the person would be given a decent burial. But we read that Joseph of Arimathea, who was a rich man and a follower of Jesus, asked for and was given the body of Jesus. This was a very brave act. The disciples had deserted Jesus, but this man was courageous and showed his courage by asking Pilate for Christ's body, which he took and placed in his own tomb — the one he had prepared for the day of his own death. At a time when most had deserted Christ, Joseph and Nicodemus came forward, so confessing to the world that they were his followers. The tomb, which had never held a dead body, was cut into rock. Christ was buried in a rich man's tomb. The prophecy of Isaiah was fulfilled.

But there is one other point we ought to notice: it is that the humiliation of Christ was now at an end. He died between criminals, but now that the salvation of his people was accomplished he was to be exalted. There was no pauper's grave for Christ. The heavenly throne of a king awaited him. And the resurrection was only a few days away. Very soon the universe would have a risen Saviour. In the burial of Christ we see the first step in the chain of events leading to his triumphant return to the glory of heaven.

One day — unless Christ returns beforehand — you and I will die and be buried. Our bodies will return to the dust. But when Jesus Christ returns he will raise our bodies from that dust and change them into glorious bodies like his (see Philippians 3:21). What a wonderful day awaits all who belong to Jesus Christ!

Activities

● ●

1. Where was Christ buried?
2. What is meant by the word 'resurrection'?
3. When will our resurrection take place?
4. What did Jesus mean when he shouted, 'It is finished'?

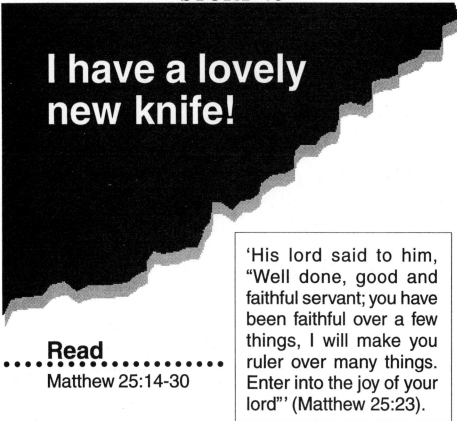

I have a lovely new knife!

Read
Matthew 25:14-30

'His lord said to him, "Well done, good and faithful servant; you have been faithful over a few things, I will make you ruler over many things. Enter into the joy of your lord"' (Matthew 25:23).

When I was young I loved adventure stories about the sea. *Treasure Island* by Robert Louis Stevenson was one of my favourites. When reading those books I imagined that I was there with the characters, doing what they did. There is no doubt that books open up a whole new world to the reader. Maybe you also like to let your imagination run wild when you are reading.

In our Bibles we read much about the new heavens and the new earth that God will make for his people. The descriptions are wonderful. But even when we try to imagine the glory that awaits each of Christ's people our minds cannot really take in very much of what it will be like. The apostle Paul put it this way:

Eye has not seen, nor ear heard,
Nor have entered into the heart of man
The things which God has prepared for those who love him
(1 Corinthians 2:9).

Now our reading and text teach us that on the Day of Judgement God will reward his people for their faithfulness. We do not deserve any reward for what we do, but the grace of God is such that rewards will flow to the saints on that great day of the Lord. I wonder what is in store for you?

A young man I have come to know recently had some experiences as a boy that I would have enjoyed very much. His mum and dad had a sailing ship and in it the family and several others sailed the world. They visited parts of the world that most of us can only read about. He has seen things that I shall never see. He has done things that I wish that I could have done. He has climbed the rigging of a sailing ship. He has slept in a bunk in a ship's cabin. He has been at sea during violent storms. In fact he had a small part in a film that has been seen around the world. The sailing ship had a big role to play in that particular film.

But this young man told me that life wasn't all fun and games. There was a lot of work to be done on the ship. Decks were to be washed down and the boat had to be kept clean. Sometimes he had to climb up the rigging to work with the sails. He used to raise and lower the flag. At other times he had jobs to do below deck. Many of them involved getting into small and dirty places. He even took his turn as watch, making sure the ship didn't strike any objects floating about on the sea.

His dad told him that he had to learn the ropes by doing jobs that he thought were not very important. In fact the young man told me that his nickname in those days was 'the Bilge Rat'. But he knew that if he did these boring or unpleasant jobs well, he would eventually be rewarded and given more responsibility and someone else would be given the less pleasant tasks to do.

On that particular ship each of the sailors wore a knife attached to his belt. I suppose the knife was used to cut ropes if an emergency arose. Maybe

154

it would also be used for scaling the fish. The young boy knew that if he did well at his work he too would in time be given a knife to wear. That would be the sign of being a good sailor. So he worked on, doing the dirty jobs that were handed out to him. Many of the tasks he didn't like doing, but as he worked he thought of the knife that one day his father would give him. I know that he also did the jobs because he loved his mother and father.

The day eventually came when he had proved his worth. He was old enough to be trusted with a knife and his parents knew that he had earned the right to wear one on his belt, just as the other sailors on the boat did. When he strapped his knife onto his belt, he felt so proud. Everything he had done to earn the right to wear a knife seemed really worthwhile. He was now looked upon by the other sailors as one of them. No longer was he 'the Bilge Rat'. Because he was the youngest on board he still had to do some of the dirty jobs, but now he did them with his knife strapped to his belt.

Our Bible reading for today tells us plainly that Christ has given each one of us talents to use in his service. We must all find out what our particular abilities are and then use them in the service of the Lord Jesus. When we do this we are simply doing what God expects of us. But today's parable teaches us that God rewards all who faithfully use the talents and opportunities given to them.

A great reward awaits each one of Christ's people. God's rewards will differ according to the way we have used his gifts. So let us each be faithful, serving God from the heart and then we shall hear those wonderful words addressed to us: 'Well done, good and faithful servant... Enter into the joy of your Lord.'

Activities

●●●

1. How does Jesus reward faithfulness?
2. Read 1 Corinthians 2:9. What does it mean? Learn the verse by heart.
3. What talents do you have to use in the service of Jesus Christ?

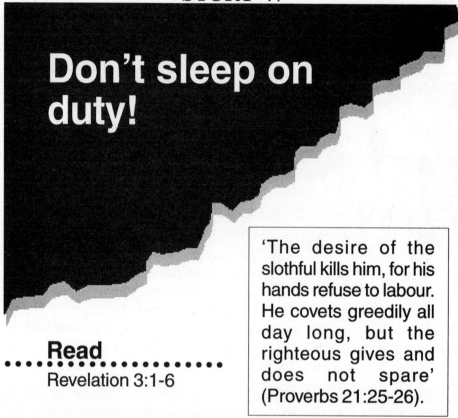

Don't sleep on duty!

Read
Revelation 3:1-6

'The desire of the slothful kills him, for his hands refuse to labour. He covets greedily all day long, but the righteous gives and does not spare' (Proverbs 21:25-26).

We all enjoy a good sleep, but there is a time to sleep and a time to be awake — wide awake! When you are tired then bed is the best place to be, but when you are playing sports you must be wide awake. Unfortunately there are some people who are plain lazy and don't want to do anything. All they want in life is to take it easy, accept no responsibility and be given everything for nothing.

Our text for today is a proverb describing lazy people. These are the people who don't want to work. They may now and again do something, but only when all else fails. They want the good things of life, but make no effort to earn them. They want to sit down to a fine meal, yet are unwilling to work for it. The slothful person is the one who longs to live in a fine house, own a fast car, dress in nice clothes and have a lot of money in the bank, and yet is unwilling to take his hands out of his pockets and get to work. And such people will die without achieving any of the things their hearts desire.

Some of these people give the impression that they are hard workers. They have a lot to say for themselves. They are always talking about what they intend to do, but never get on with actually doing it.

We all need to remember that we have a God-given obligation to work. The commandment tells us, 'Six days you shall labour and do all your work...' (Exodus 20:9).

I would like to tell you another story concerning the young man I wrote about in my last story. His name is Matthew and a fine man he is. You will recall that he spent most of his younger days sailing the world with his family. I also told you that he was given many jobs to do, some of which he didn't like.

One job that he was given on occasions was to keep watch on the bow of the ship. He would have a one-hour shift watching the ocean for any objects that might smash a hole in the boat. This was an important job as there are many dangerous objects floating on the waves. Large logs are washed out to sea in times of flood and they can do a lot of damage to boats. Also containers are often washed overboard from the large cargo

ships that sail the seas. These containers sometimes float just at the surface of the water. If a wooden boat smashed into one of them a hole could be torn in its hull.

Keeping watch was therefore a most important job. Matthew's dad told him to stand up and keep watch. By standing up there would be no chance of his going to sleep and failing in his duty.

On one particular watch the ship was sailing along very smoothly, so Matthew sat down. As there seemed to be nothing at all floating about on the sea, he found a lovely cosy place in the warm sun and from there he tried to keep watch. I'm sure you can guess what happened — Matthew fell asleep. As it turned out the boat came to no harm while he was asleep, but he told me that suddenly he felt a hard slap on the shoulder. Then a sailor began to shake him and dragged him to his feet.

'You are supposed to be on watch!' the sailor shouted. 'Get on your feet and take notice of what is happening. Anything could be floating about on the ocean. You do your duty! Don't you dare sit down and go to sleep on watch — ever!'

Matthew got the message: laziness, or sloth, would not be tolerated on board his father's ship. He knew that failing to keep watch could cause a serious accident at sea. Never again did he sit down during his time on watch.

Now we need to beware of laziness in our daily lives. While we are at school we should work hard at our studies and help our parents in jobs around the home. When we grow up we must work for our wages and then use them for good purposes. We must provide for our families, as well as supporting the work of the church. Our giving helps spread the gospel. And we must always be ready to help those who are in genuine need.

As professing Christians we have a work to do. Christians are not called to spiritual laziness. Jesus told his hearers, 'Strive to enter through the narrow gate...' (Luke 13:24). Humanly speaking, becoming a Christian is not easy. It means you must turn away from the sins you love to a life of righteousness. You may have to give up your godless friends who would hinder your Christian growth. You may have a special friend you hope one day to marry, but that friend is not a Christian. Christians are not to marry non-Christians.

Becoming a Christian calls for many sacrifices. Christianity means work — not laziness. You will devote time to prayer and the reading of your Bible. You will keep Sunday as a holy day, and give time to worship God with your fellow Christians. The person who claims to be a Christian but does not live as a Christian is nothing more than a hypocrite. The destiny of such people is certainly not heaven, unless they repent.

Today's reading is the letter to the church at Sardis, which had the reputation of being very much alive, but in fact was almost dead. The members of that church were called to repent of their sin of slothfulness. They were not faithful people doing the work that Christ commanded them to do.

So, reader, where do you stand today concerning your spiritual life? Are you a lazy professing Christian or one who delights to do the works of God? Always remember what the Lord Jesus Christ said — and these are frightening words when you think long and hard about them: 'Not everyone who says to me, "Lord, Lord," shall enter the kingdom of heaven, but he who does the will of my Father in heaven' (Matthew 7:21). No one will ever sleep their way into paradise.

Activities

● ●

1. Explain what today's text means.
2. Why are we all to work?
3. Whom should Christians marry? Why?
4. Read Matthew 7:21 and discuss what the passage teaches.

Keep your eyes upon Jesus

.... Read ....
Matthew 14:22-33

'Let us run with endurance the race that is set before us, looking unto Jesus, the author and finisher of our faith...' (Hebrews 12:1-2).

Christians are people who look to Jesus for their salvation.

To be successful in the things of this life we need to keep our minds on what we are doing. When I take a hammer to drive a nail into timber I always carefully watch what I am doing. I know that if I take my eyes off the nail I could hit anything — most likely my thumb. When I measure medicine I carefully watch what I am doing.

Many years ago I took a class on an excursion to a steelworks. We had to travel three hours each way by bus. The children read books, talked to each other, sang songs and some even became travel-sick. But when we reached the city area everyone began to gaze at the scenes outside the bus windows.

It wasn't long before we arrived at the first set of traffic lights. (There are no traffic lights in the town in which we all lived.) The lights turned red

just as we were approaching them. As the bus slowed down all the children looked about them. They saw a milkman pushing along a barrow of bottled milk. He was being very careful as he walked along. I'm sure he didn't want to break any bottles. He was watching the pathway to make sure the wheels of the barrow didn't bump into anything. When the bus came to a halt, the kids on the bus called out, 'G'day mate!'

The fellow took his eyes off the pathway and gave the children in the bus a big smile. They all returned his smile and some waved to him. Without thinking he took one hand off the barrow and returned the wave. As he did so one wheel struck a rock on the pathway and the barrow capsized. All the milk bottles toppled onto the cement pathway, breaking into thousands of pieces. I felt embarrassed as the children burst out laughing at the poor fellow.

The moral to the story is: don't take your eyes off the job you are doing. If you do anything can happen.

Today's reading is about the Lord Jesus walking across the sea. The disciples had set off earlier in a boat and now, after a time of prayer, Jesus was coming after them. The sea was rough and the boat was being tossed about. When the disciples saw Christ coming towards them, walking on the waves, they were terrified. They wondered what the figure on the water could be.

As soon as he realized that it was the Lord, Peter stepped out of the boat to walk towards him, as Christ had invited him to do. Peter knew that Christ's power could support him as he walked across the water. Everything went well while Peter kept his eyes upon Jesus. But as soon as he took his eyes off Jesus he saw the rough waves round about him and began to sink in the water. His faith failed him when he looked away from Jesus.

In our Christian lives we must always keep our eyes upon Jesus. We do this by reading our Bibles, spending time in prayer and mixing with the people of God. As soon as Christians start to pay attention to the things of the world their faith is weakened and their spiritual life begins to falter. We all need to keep our spiritual eyes upon Jesus.

In Isaiah 45:22 we read wonderful words : 'Look to me, and be saved, all you ends of the earth! For I am God, and there is no other.' Christian, keep your spiritual eyes upon God in Christ! Keep looking upwards and glorify God in all that you do and say. If you continue to do this you will not backslide but remain faithful to the Saviour.

Activities

●●

1. Why did Peter sink into the water when he walked towards Jesus?
2. What do you think it means when we are told to keep our eyes upon Jesus?
3. Who is the only true God?
4. Is Jesus Christ God? How do you know?

A great fire alarm!

Read
....
Luke 23:32-47

'In this the love of God was manifested toward us, that God has sent his only begotten Son into the world, that we might live through him' (1 John 4:9).

Unsaved people have no real understanding of God's great love towards sinners. Anyone who does not have a personal experience of the love of God as seen in the person of Jesus Christ has a very poor life indeed. But all those who are born of God's Holy Spirit have experienced God's love. They, in their turn, should be filled with love towards God and towards all others, especially those people who are their brothers and sisters in Christ.

Christian love is a love that not only floods the heart, but is seen in the works done in the name of Jesus Christ. And God's love is just that — love in action.

It is impossible to understand how God could love sinners. We are all sinners, born with a sinful nature, and because of this nature we willingly sin. We break God's holy law and do not want to come to the Lord Jesus Christ for salvation. But God loved sinners. For this reason he determined to save a people through the work of the Lord Jesus Christ, his only begotten Son. God's love is great and beyond understanding.

Occasionally we hear of some great act of love and I want to tell you of a case that I heard about.

I don't like fires. Every summer Australia suffers from bush fires and there is much damage done to the countryside. Also there seem to be a lot more house fires than before. Every home-owner is now being urged to fit electronic smoke detectors. We have three in our home now. We have put them in places where they will give us plenty of warning if a fire breaks out.

One day we saw a television news-report about a house fire. The home-owner and his wife were being interviewed beside the remains of their house. They were both in tears and my first thought was that they were upset by the loss of their home. But this was only part of the reason why they were crying. Between tears and sobs the woman said that the first they knew of the fire was the warning bark of their pet dog. The dog had smelt the smoke and was concerned for the safety of his owners. So he began barking loudly and woke them.

The husband and wife were able to escape without any injury. But once outside they realized that the dog was still inside the house. Despite their efforts to get to him, the fierce flames drove them back and the little dog died in the flames. The couple spoke of their love for the pet dog who had saved their lives. They praised their brave little friend and said they would never be able to replace him.

I tried to imagine how they must have felt, but as no pet dog has ever died for me it was difficult for me to have any real sense of the grief that filled their hearts. They loved their pet now more than ever.

Reader, if you have been saved by the life and death of the Lord Jesus Christ you have experienced the greatest love in the universe. God loved us while we were rebellious sinners. So great was his love for his people that he willingly gave his Son to save them.

Christ humbled himself and came into the world in sinless flesh and blood. He had a true human nature. He lived among sinners who ill-treated him terribly. Yet he willingly laid down his life on the cross and bore the fierce anger of God that was due to his people because of their sins. He died so that his people might live with him for ever.

If you are saved then remember the words of the apostle John: 'We love him because he first loved us' (1 John 4:19). One great reason for loving God is because he saved us through the work of his Son, Jesus Christ.

But there is a second reason for loving God and that is because of his character. The Christian is a new creature who is being moulded in the likeness of Christ. Our God is the all-wise God of grace, love, mercy and perfect justice. He is a caring God who works all things for his glory and the benefit of his people. Our God is good in all he does and he is holy in all his ways. (*The Shorter Catechism* says in answer to the question, 'What is God?': 'God is a Spirit, infinite, eternal, and unchangeable, in his being, wisdom, power, holiness, justice, goodness, and truth.') Should you not love this glorious God simply because of his character?

If you have experienced God's love give him thanks for your salvation and then show your love by obedience to his commandments. Seek to love him with all your heart, soul, mind and body and glorify him in all you do, say and think.

Activities

●●●

1. How did God show his great love to sinners?
2. Why do Christians love God?
3. How do Christians show that they love God?

How is your heart beating?

Read
Mark 7:14-23

> 'The heart is deceitful above all things, and desperately wicked; who can know it? I, the LORD, search the heart, I test the mind...' (Jeremiah 17:9-10).

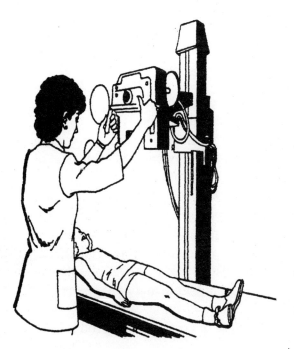

Recently my mother broke her arm. At first she was not sure if she had broken it as she didn't have X-ray eyesight. However, the doctor sent her to the radiologist and the X-ray detected the break. The machine could see into the body. Now this is certainly a marvellous machine.

After an accident some years ago I developed extreme pain in the back. A special machine was able to look through my skin and showed up a lump on a spinal disc. This machine was more sensitive than the ordinary

X-ray. After surgery I was still experiencing a lot of pain so I returned to the specialist who arranged for a test called 'magnetic resonance imaging' to be done on my back. The machine that did the testing was able to show even the tissues in my spine. The doctors could clearly see scar tissue — the result of the back surgery.

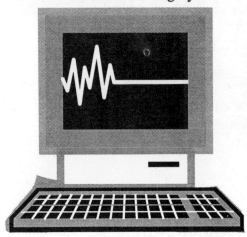

I'm sure my grandfather, who died forty years ago, would have told me, 'No machine will ever be able to see what is going on inside the body. They'll never invent a machine to do that.' But he would have been wrong.

And what about our hearts? My wife was told by the doctor that she would need some special testing of her heart to measure her heartbeat and blood pressure over a period of time. So some electrodes were placed on her chest with a blood pressure testing wrapper placed around her arm. Everything was connected to a small computer that she carried in a bag over her shoulder. Every half-hour the machine took her blood pressure and checked her heartbeat. The next day the doctor was able to tell her what had been happening in her heart. I never cease to be amazed by inventions that tell us more about ourselves.

But they haven't invented a machine (at least I don't think so) to reveal what goes on in my thoughts. Like you, I have some thoughts I would not like anyone to know about.

Our text tells us that God is able to look into our hearts and minds. He knows our thoughts. He knows the reason for everything we do. God knows more about you and me than we know about ourselves. This is frightening, but it also can be wonderful. God knows every one of our sins — even our sinful thoughts. He also knows the reason behind our sins. There are times when we fail in doing good — not because we intend to fail, but because things don't work out as we planned. When that happens it is wonderful to know that God has already seen that we had the right intention.

The great problem with sinners is the state of their hearts. Today's reading explains this very clearly. In verses 20-23 we read Christ's words: 'What comes out of a man, that defiles a man. For from within, out of the heart of men, proceed evil thoughts, adulteries, fornications, murders, thefts, covetousness, wickedness, deceit, licentiousness, an evil eye, blasphemy, pride, foolishness. All these things come from within and defile a man.'

The Pharisees were concerned that Christ's disciples were eating their food without first washing their hands. Now of course it is a good idea to wash your hands before eating. This helps get rid of the germs that could affect your health. But the Pharisees were not worried about the health of Christ's disciples. They believed that the disciples were making themselves spiritually unclean by eating with unwashed hands. The Jews considered the Gentiles to be spiritually unclean. They believed that the Gentiles had no part in God's kingdom. The Pharisees, then, accused Christ's disciples of eating without washing their hands, not because their hands were dirty but because they had come from a public place where they had come into contact with Gentiles.

But Jesus knew the real problem with humans — a sinful heart. In the heart, or the mind, sinful thoughts arose. Then so often those sinful thoughts were put into action and the evils mentioned in our reading followed. What is needed as far as sinners are concerned is a heart transplant. The sinful heart of stone needs to be replaced with a spiritual heart of flesh (Ezekiel 36:26-27). Only God can do this. Jesus said that sinners had to be born again if they were to see God and enter heaven. This is the gracious work of the Holy Spirit (John 3:1-8).

Reader, are you born again? If so, give thanks to God for that wonderful work of grace. But if not, then pray earnestly that God might send his Spirit to convict you of your sins, give you the gift of saving faith and a love for himself.

Activities

● ●

1. Which part of a person is most wicked?
2. How does God bring about a change in the sinner's heart?
3. We are told that the Holy Spirit convicts people of their sins. What does this mean?
4. What is sin and why is it so terrible?

Get rid of the rats!

Read . . . .
Galatians 1:6-12

'There is a way which seems right to a man, but its end is the way of death' (Proverbs 14:12).

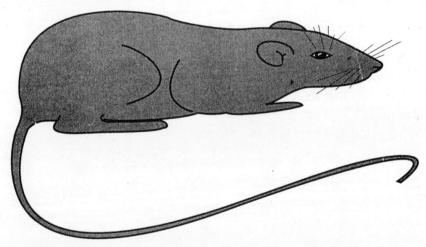

Jim, a very good friend of mine, is terrified of rats. He hates the sight of them and will have nothing to do with them. The closest he now comes to a rat is when he has to get a dead one out of a trap. He told me why he is frightened of rats and it went something like this.

Jim used to spend a lot of his spare time working in his garage. But he noticed evidence of mice and rats. He set some traps but all he caught were small mice. One evening as he was working he heard a noise in the corner of the garage. When he looked he said he saw the biggest rat he had ever seen.

Now in those days Jim was very brave as far as rats were concerned. He grabbed a broom and quietly moved towards the big rat thinking he would easily get rid of the creature. But suddenly the rat looked at him and realized it was cornered. Jim said that it stood up on its hind legs and snarled at him. Then just as he brought the broom down the rat jumped at his leg, bit him on the ankle and escaped. Ever since that day Jim has been terrified of rats.

I don't like rats or mice either, but sometimes we hear them in the ceiling of the house. How they get in I don't know. The builder told me he put mesh wire around the foundations to prevent such animals getting into the house.

One night our daughter Lisa ran into our bedroom and said she could hear noises in the ceiling. She was scared by the sounds and soon the three of us were in the bed quietly listening. Then we heard them! Valerie said they sounded like a herd of elephants running across the ceiling. The decision was made that they had to be exterminated.

I visited a shop that sold a rat poison mixture and was told to put some poison in dishes in the space above the ceiling. After buying a supply I asked the shop assistant how strong the poison was. He told me a little about it. The most interesting part of the information was that almost all of the rat mixture was made up of harmless foods rats love to eat. In fact he claimed that 99% of the rat poison mixture wouldn't hurt anything. But, he went on to say, 'It's the 1% of deadly poison that does the job. That small bit of poison will kill a rat or mouse in no time at all.'

I then went home and carefully placed dishes of rat poison in the space above the ceiling. Within days we heard no more sounds of mice running across the ceiling. Lisa went back to her own bed. Every now and again I put a little more poison in the dishes and since that date we have had no trouble with rodents in the house. But think about that poisonous mixture — 99% good to eat and just 1% that did the job of killing.

Now our reading for today comes from the book of Galatians where we are told that Paul was having trouble with the Jews. He had been preaching that sinners were saved by faith in Christ — and that alone. He taught that there was nothing a sinner could do to win favour with God. No, God's favour had been won for his people by Jesus Christ. After a sinner was saved obedience followed, out of love for the Saviour. But that obedience did not save anyone.

Some of the Jews who were troublemakers began to teach that it was good to have faith in Christ, but if sinners wanted to be saved they had first of all to be circumcised — that is, they had to become Jews. So the pure gospel was now mixed with error. And Paul warned the Christians that this mixture would lead to death. Paul always taught that sinners were saved without the works of the law. There was nothing wrong with circumcision. In fact Paul ordered Timothy to be circumcised so that the Jews would accept him as one of themselves (Acts 16:3). In this way Timothy would be able to mix freely with the Jews and preach the gospel to them.

When good deeds are added to faith in Christ as necessary for salvation, the result is spiritual death. No doubt many Jews in Paul's day thought the gospel they preached of faith in Christ and obedience to the law was good and proper. But good works mixed with faith in Christ were no longer the gospel as taught by the apostle Paul.

Paul then said of those people who were preaching a different message: 'But even if we, or an angel from heaven, preach any other gospel to you than what we have preached to you, let him be accursed' (Galatians 1:8).

Today we have men and women who claim to be ministers of Christ but really are servants of Satan. They preach that there are a lot of different ways to be saved. 'Just do the right thing and God will smile on you,' they claim. Some even argue, 'You must speak in tongues in order to be saved.' Many follow these people, but they are eating spiritual poison.

Reader, get your Bible open and be like those noble Bereans! (see Acts 17:10-12). Check out against the Word of God what your pastor preaches from the pulpit. Don't be led astray by blind guides. God's people are saved through faith in Christ — nothing else. And that saving faith is the free gift of a gracious God. Praise God!

Activities

• •

1. Describe the way that leads to eternal life.
2. Why was Timothy circumcised? (See Acts 16:3).
3. The Bereans are praised. Why?

One that didn't get away!

Read
Matthew 19:16-26

'And Jesus said to him, "Assuredly, I say to you, today you will be with me in Paradise"' (Luke 23:43).

As you will know if you have read any of my other books, my brother John and I always used to enjoy a day's fishing. It is great to get away from everything for a time and just sit and dangle a line in the water. Fishing out at sea is a wonderful experience and there is always a chance of catching a big fish.

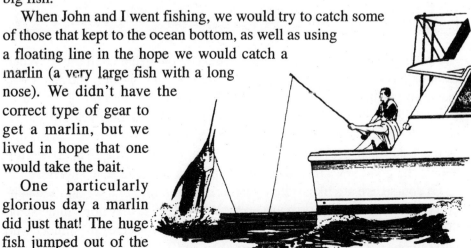

When John and I went fishing, we would try to catch some of those that kept to the ocean bottom, as well as using a floating line in the hope we would catch a marlin (a very large fish with a long nose). We didn't have the correct type of gear to get a marlin, but we lived in hope that one would take the bait.

One particularly glorious day a marlin did just that! The huge fish jumped out of the water, stood upright and skimmed across the surface of the ocean. Then it splashed into a wave and headed for the wide open spaces. The line raced through our hands and soon our 500 metres of nylon came to an end and the huge fish just broke the line and kept going. John and I were very disappointed to see the fish escape, but now we can tell everyone of 'the one that got away' — a two- or three-metre monster.

As the day passed we caught some large snapper which search out food on the ocean bottom. We lost one big fish, but at the end of the day we returned home with several bags full of fish — as well as Val's clothes-basket overflowing. When you go fishing you catch some and others escape. But if no fish were caught trip after trip I'm sure fishermen would give up and take up another sport.

Jesus called his disciples to be fishermen — but fishers of humans. When Jesus called Peter and Andrew to follow him he said, 'Follow me, and I will make you fishers of men' (Matthew 4:19). Every Christian is called to confess Christ. In this way Christians are fishermen as they want to 'catch' people for Jesus. We want to see people becoming followers of Christ. Just as the fisherman uses bait to attract the attention of the fish, so we tell people the good news that Jesus came into the world to save sinners.

Of course, we are like ordinary fishermen and find that we don't 'catch' every person for Jesus. Some just go their own way, as they don't understand they have a need of a Saviour. But others see themselves as sinners who will only be saved if they trust themselves to Christ.

Our Scripture text and reading for today record the outcome of what happened when two men came into contact with Jesus. The reading is about that rich young man who wanted eternal life. I'm sure he meant what he said. But when he discovered that he would have to sacrifice everything and follow Jesus, he went away unsaved. He loved the things of the world more than he did eternal life.

But then our text concerns a thief on a cross. This man was dying a horrible death. He was hanging on a cross alongside that of Jesus. There on the cross the dying thief recognized Jesus as the King of Israel. I am always amazed when I read this story. Jesus didn't look like a king of any kind as he hung upon that cross. But the Holy Spirit touched the thief's heart and he saw what others could not see. He saw Jesus as the Son of God who saves sinners. Our text is Christ's reply to this man, telling him that he would be with Jesus in paradise. Wasn't that a wonderful answer?

A fisherman would say that the rich young man was 'the one that got away'. But the thief on the cross was caught. He didn't get away.

Now my friend, have you been 'caught' by the gospel of Christ? Are you one of Christ's disciples? If you are, then you have become one of Christ's fishermen. So get on with the job Christ has given you. Make sure you live a godly life and use your life and words to attract sinners to Christ. And pray that God might touch the hearts of the people to whom you witness and bring them to Christ.

Maybe you are 'the one that got away'. If so, pray that God will show you mercy so that you might come to saving faith in Jesus Christ, his beloved Son.

Activities

● ●

1. To whom did Jesus say, 'Today you will be with me in paradise'?
2. What did our Lord mean when he spoke about 'paradise'?
3. How do you go about trying to 'catch' someone for Jesus?

If you have been spiritually blessed by what you have read in this book, please send a postcard of your home town to:

Jim Cromarty
3 Appaloosa Place
Wingham
NSW 2429
Australia